Machine Learning

A Beginners Guide to Machine Learning

KEVIN BRIAN

© Copyright 2021 (KEVIN BRIAN) –All rights are reserved.

taken.

The cause for this paper is to provide accurate and

authentic information on the subject and problem covered. The reporting is sold because the publisher is not required to provide eligible accounting services, either officially permit or otherwise. Judicial or technical advice, if relevant, then should order it from a practiced individual in the profession.

The Declaration of Principles was acquiring and favorably by the American Bar Association Committee and the Publishers and company Committee.

It is not allowed, in any way, to copy, replicate, or issue any portion of this document in any electronic or printed form. Recording this document is strictly forbidden, and this document's protection is not allowed unless the publisher has written consent to do so. All rights are taken.

The information presented herein is supposed to be precise and stable. In the event of distraction or otherwise, any responsibility, use, or misuse of any rules, procedure, or command found therein shall be the recipient reader's sole and absolute control. Under no condition will any civil responsibility be imposed on the publisher, either directly or indirectly, for reparation, damages, or monetary loss due to the information found therein.

Respective writers own all copyrights that the publisher does not own.

The information given herein is for informative purposes only and is universal as such. The presentation of the story is without a contract or any guarantee of assurance.

The trademarks used are without any consent, and the publication of the trademark is without permission or backing by the trademark owner. This book's trademarks and brands are for clarifying purposes only and are owned themselves, not affiliated with this document.

Table of Contents

Introduction 4

Chapter 1: The Basics of Machine Learning (ML) 5

    1.1: History of Machine Learning 9

    1.2: How Does Machine Learning Work? 13

    1.3: Companies Which are Using Machine Learning 16

Chapter 2: Find Your Machine Learning Tribe 20

    2.1: Pick a Tool for Machine Learning for Beginners 29

    2.2: Pick a Tool for Machine Learning for Intermediate 40

    2.3: Pick a Tool for Advanced Machine Learning 47

    2.4: Best Programming Languages for Machine Learning 54

Chapter 3: Practice on Database 57

    3.1: Build a Machine Learning Portfolio 67

    3.2: Get Paid to Apply Machine Learning 71

    3.3: Machine Learning for Money 75

Chapter 4: Applied Machine Learning Process 78

    4.1: Prepare Your Data 81

    4.2: Spot-Check Algorithm 92

    4.3: Improve Results 101

Chapter 5: Advantages and Disadvantages of Machine Learning 108

    5.1: Benefits of Machine Learning 109

    5.2: Disadvantages of Machine Learning 115

Conclusion 116

Introduction

Machine learning (ML) is a type of artificial intelligence (AI) that enables software applications to predict results without being directly programmed. Machine learning algorithms use historical data as input to predict new output values.

Engines of suggestion are a typical case for machine learning use. Other expected benefits include identifying fraud, spam filtering, detecting malware attacks, automation of business processes (BPA), and predictive maintenance.

Classical machine learning is also characterized by how an algorithm in its forecasts learns to become more precise. Four foundational methods are available: supervised learning, unsupervised learning, semi-supervised learning, and reinforcement learning. The algorithm that a data scientist prefers to use depends on the knowledge they choose to forecast.

They are learning under observation. Data scientists provide algorithms with named training data in machine learning and specify the variables they want the algorithm to test for correlations. The algorithm's input and output are all defined.

They are learning unsupervised. Algorithms that train on unlabeled data are used in this form of machine learning — the algorithm scans for some significant relation through data sets. The data algorithms are educating on both, and the forecasts or suggestions they make are predetermined.

They are learning semi-supervised. A combination of the two previous forms includes this approach to machine learning. Data scientists can feed mainly named training data to an algorithm, but the model is free to explore the data independently and establish its knowledge of the data collection.

They are learning Reinforcement. Typically, reinforcement learning is used to train a computer to complete a multi-step procedure within which explicitly defined rules exist. To achieve a task, data scientists program an algorithm and send it positive or negative signals while it figures out how to finish a job. But the algorithm chooses on its own what steps to take along the way, for the most part.

To keep things simple, just know that by finding patterns in similar data, machines "learn." Think of data as information from the world that you acquire. The more data that is given to a computer, the "smarter" it gets.

Although not all the data is similar, imagine that you are a pirate, and your life's mission was to find somewhere on the island a buried treasure. You will need a sufficient amount of data to find the treasure. Like knowledge, this data will either lead you in the correct direction or the wrong direction. The higher the data/data that is collected, the smaller the uncertainty, and vice versa. So it's essential to keep in mind the kind of information you give your machine to learn.

Chapter 1: The Basics of Machine Learning (ML)

A significant feature of current business and analysis is Machine Learning (ML). To allow computer systems to enhance their performance increases, it uses algorithms and neural network models. "Algorithms in Machine Learning automatically create a mathematical model using sample data to make decisions without being directly programmed to make those decisions, also known as "training data.

In part, Machine Learning is base on a brain cell interaction model. Donald Hebb introduced the model in 1949 in a book entitled The Organization of Actions (PDF). Hebb's ideas on neuron excitement and contact between neurons are discussed in the book.

As one cell regularly assists in firing another, Hebb wrote, the axon of the first cell produces synaptic knobs in contact with the second cell's soma (or enlarges them if they already exist). His model can be defined as a way to modify the relationships between artificial neurons (also referred to as nodes) and individual neurons' changes by translating Hebb's principles to artificial neural networks and artificial neurons. If all neurons/nodes are activated simultaneously, the bond between two neurons/nodes strengthens and weakens if they are simultaneously activated. The term "weight" is used to characterize these relationships, and nodes/neurons that appear positive or negative describe having strong positive weights. Strong negative weights are developed by certain nodes tending to have opposite weights.

The Game of Checkers Machine Learning

Arthur Samuel of IBM created computer software for playing checkers in the 1950s. Since the software had a minimal amount of usable machine memory, what is called alpha-beta pruning was introduced by Samuel. A scoring mechanism using the locations of the pieces on the board was used in his concept. The scoring feature tried to quantify the probability of each side winning. Using a minimax technique, which ultimately developed into the minimax algorithm, the computer selects the next move.

Samuel also developed a variety of methods to allow his software to get better. His software recorded/remembered all positions that it had already seen and coupled this with the reward function values in what Samuel called rote learning. In 1952, Arthur Samuel first came up with the term "Machine Learning."

The Perceptions

In 1957, at the Cornell Aeronautical Laboratory, Frank Rosenblatt coupled the brain cell interaction model of Donald Hebb with the Machine Learning efforts of Arthur Samuel and developed the perceptron. As a computer, not a program, the perceptron was initially designed. Initially created for the IBM 704, the device integrated into a custom-made computer built for image recognition called the Mark 1 perceptron.

She was described as the first successful neuro-computer; this made the program and the algorithms transferable to other computers and made them usable.

Some problems with broken expectations created the Mark I perceptron. Although the perceptron appeared promising, many visual patterns could not be recognized, causing frustration and stalling research on the neural network. It will be many years before taxpayers' and financing agencies' grievances disappeared. Neural Network/Machine Learning experiments suffered during the 1990s before a revival.

The Algorithm for the Closest Neighbor

The nearest neighbor algorithm, which was the beginning of simple pattern recognition, was invented in 1967. This algorithm was used to map routes and was one of the first algorithms used in seeking a solution to the problem of finding the most suitable path for the traveling salesperson. A salesperson visits a chosen city using it and makes the software hit the closest cities repeatedly before they have been reached. Credit has been given to Marcello Pelillo for inventing the "nearest neighbor law." In turn, he credits the famous 1967 Cover and Hart Paper.

Provide the next step with Multilayers

In the 1960s, in neural network science, multilayers' invention and use opened a new direction. The supply and service of two or three layers in the perceptron provided considerably more computing power than a perceptron using one sheet. Since the perceptron opened the door to 'layers' in networks, other iterations of neural networks were developed, and the diversity of neural networks continues to grow. The use of many layers has contributed to neural feedforward networks and backpropagation.

Built-in the 1970s, backpropagation enables a network to change its hidden neuron/node layers to respond to new scenarios. It explains "the backward propagation of errors," with an error being processed at the output and then transmitted for learning purposes backward across the layers of the network. Backpropagation is now used to train deep neural networks.

There are unseen layers of an Artificial Neural Network (ANN) used to respond to more complex tasks than the earlier perceptions. The primary method used for Machine

interesting for statisticians, it has been introduced in R" (well said). He also complains that language itself is ugly and difficult to deal with. Finally, Ben reflects on Julia, who doesn't have anything to say in libraries but is his new favorite language. He points out that it has the conciseness of languages like MATLAB and Python with C's speed.

Anthony Gold bloom, CEO of Kaggle, gave a presentation to the Bay Area R user community in 2011 on R's success at Kaggle's Predictive Modeling Competitions: Making data science a sport (see the PowerPoint slides). The declines in the presentation give more information on the use of programming languages and propose another group that is similar to as broad as the use of R. It would be great to have the raw data gathered (why didn't they disclose it to their data group, seriously!).

John Langford, on his blog, Hunch, has an excellent post on the properties of programming language to be considered while dealing with machine learning algorithms named "Programming Languages for Machine Learning Implementations." It splits the properties into questions about speed and programmability (programming ease). It points to robust industry-standard algorithm implementations, all in C, and comments that it did not use R or MATLAB (the post was wrote8 years ago). Take the time to read some of the remarks made by scholars and business experts alike. It is a complex and complicated dilemma that always boils down to the specifics of the problem you tackle and the environment in which you solve it.

Languages for Machine Learning

I am speaking about programming languages in the light of the machine learning tasks that I would like to do.

MATLAB/Octave:

I think MATLAB is excellent for describing and dealing with matrixes. As such, I think it's a perfect language or medium to use when climbing to the linear algebra of a given system. I think it's a smart idea to read about algorithms both superficially for the first time around and profoundly when you're trying to find out something or get deep into the process. For example, it's popular with beginners at university, including Andrew Ng's Coursera Machine Learning course.

R

R is a workhorse for mathematical analysis and deep learning by extension. There's a lot of talk about the learning curve, and I didn't see the issue. It is the tool to be used to explain and analyze the data using mathematical tools and graphs. It has an overwhelming number of machines learning algorithms and specialized applications written by algorithm developers.

You can investigate, model, and build with R. I think it fits one-off projects with artifacts like a compilation of projections, analyses, or academic papers. It is, for example, the most common forum for machine learning competitors such as Kaggle.

Python

Python is a popular scientific language and a rising star for machine learning. I would be shocked if the data analysis mantle from R could use. Still, matrix handling in NumPy could challenge MATLAB, and collaboration methods like I Python are very enticing and a step towards the future of reproducibility.

The SciPy stack for machine learning and data processing should use for one-off experiments (including papers), and applications like sci-kit-learn are mature enough to be used in production systems.

Java-family

The implementation of a framework that uses machine learning is a technical problem like any other. You need a good concept, and you need to have developed specifications. Machine learning is not sorcery but algorithms. When it comes to serious production implementations, you need a sound library or configure the algorithm to suit your needs.

For example, there are robust libraries, and Java has Weka and Mahout. Notice also that more in-depth implementations of key algorithms such as regression (LIBLINEAR) and SVM (LIBSVM) are written in C and leveraged by Python and other toolkits. I assume you're serious about being a prototype in R or Python. Still, you're going to introduce it in a more decadent language for reasons such as ease of execution and machine stability. E.g., the BigML backend is implemented in Clojure.

Other Consideration

Not a programmer: If you are not a programmer (or not a confident programmer), I suggest that you play machine learning through a GUI interface like Weka.

One Vocabulary of Study and Ops: You will want to use the same vocabulary for prototyping and development to minimize the chance of not successfully translating the findings.

Pet Language: You might have your favorite language's pet language, and you want to stick to it. You should set up algorithms yourself or use libraries. Most languages have some type of machine learning package, however fundamental it may be.

Chapter 3: Practice on Database

Where do you find the best datasets for studying machine learning? Datasets that are real-world in such a way that they are fascinating and important, albeit tiny enough for you to review in Excel and work from your laptop.

In this part, you can find a directory of high-quality, real-world, and well-understood machine learning datasets that you can use to practice applied machine learning.

This archive is called the UCI machine learning library, and you can use it to create a self-study curriculum and build a stable framework for machine learning.

Why do we require data sets to practice?

If you are interested in studying applied machine learning, you need datasets for practicing.

It is a dilemma that will stop you dead.

Can dataset be you going to use?

Are you going to collect your own or use one off the shelf?

What one of them and why?

I teach a top-down approach to machine learning where I empower you to learn how to operate on an end-to-end task, map the process to a tool, and practice the data process in a focused manner.

How are you going to train in a targeted way?

I teach you that the easiest way to get started is to learn datasets that have unique functionality.

I suggest that you pick features that you may find and need to fix when you start working on your issues, such as:

- Various forms of supervised learning, such as grouping and regression.
- Different scale databases from tens, hundreds, thousands, even millions of cases.
- The different number of attributes of fewer than five, tens, hundreds, and thousands of attributes.
- Different types of attributes from true, integer, categorical, ordinal, and mixtures
- Multiple domains force you to rapidly grasp and describe a new challenge you have no prior experience with.

You will create a program with features to research and learn from and an algorithm that you need to solve by creating a test problem dataset program to work on.

Such a curriculum has a range of functional criteria, such as:

The Modern World: Datasets are to be taken from the real world (rather than being contrived). It will make them interesting and present the problems that come with the actual results.

Small: Databases need to be small to inspect and interpret them so you can easily run a variety of models to improve the learning time.

Well-understood: There should be a good understanding of what the data comprises, whether it was gathered, what the dilemma is that it has to be figured out so that you can frame the investigation.

Baseline: It is also important to understand what algorithms are considered to do well and the scores they have obtained such that you have a useful point of reference. It is important when you get started and practice, so you need fast input on how well you're doing (close to the state-of-the-art or something is broken).

Plentiful: You need many datasets to pick from, both to fulfill the characteristics that you would like to analyze and (if possible) your inherent curiosity and interest.

You will get anything you need and more from the UCI Machine Learning Repository in terms of datasets for beginners.

What's the UCI Machine Learning Repository?

The UCI Machine Learning Library is a collection of machines learning problems that you can use free of charge.

It is hosted and operated by the Centre for Machine Learning and Intelligent Systems, University of California, Irvine. David Aha originally developed it as a graduate student at UC Irvine.

For more than 25 years, machine-learning developers and machine-learning professionals require a dataset.

Each dataset will have its website detailing all the information known about it, including any related publications that examine it. Datasets themselves can be accessed as ASCII files, mostly in a useful CSV format.

For example, here is the Abalone Data Set web page that involves predicting the abalone age from their physical measurements.

Benefits of the depository

Many of the useful aspects of the library include:

- Almost all datasets are taken from the domain (compared to being synthetic), which ensures they have real-world attributes.
- Datasets cover a wide variety of topics, from genetics to particle physics.
- Details of datasets are outlined by factors such as attribute forms, number of cases, number of attributes, and the reported year that can be filtered and searched.
- The datasets are well studied, which means that they are well known for their intriguing properties and predicted "good" outcomes. It can provide a valuable baseline for reference.
- Most datasets are tiny (hundreds to thousands of instances), which means that you can easily load and analyze them in a text editor or MS Excel, and you can easily model them on your workstation.

Browse the 300+ datasets in this useful table that facilitates sorting and searching.

Criticism of the Repository

Some of the repository's critiques include:

- Datasets are washed, which means that researchers who prepared them have also already done some pre-processing to collect attributes and instances.
- The databases are limited, but this is not helpful if you research larger-scale problems and techniques.
- There are so many to pick from that you can freeze indecision and over-analysis. It can be hard to pick a dataset and get started because you're unsure if it's a "good dataset" for what you're investigating.
- Datasets are restricted to tabular data, mainly for classification purposes (although clustering and regression datasets are listed). It is limited to those involved in natural language, computer vision, recommendations, and other details.

Take a look at the repository dashboard as it displays the datasets featured, the latest datasets, and which datasets are currently the most common.

A curriculum of self-study

So, how do you make the most of the UCI machine learning repository?

I would encourage you to think about the problem dataset's functionality that you would like to hear about.

There could be traits that you would prefer to model (like regression) or algorithms that model certain traits that you would like to use more skillfully (like a random forest for multiclass classification).

An example program could look like the following one:

Binary Classification: Pima Indian Diabetes Data Set (available here)

Multiclass Classification: Iris Data Set

Regression: data collection on the production of wine

Classical Attributes: Breast Cancer Data Collection

Integer attributes: data collection for computer hardware

Classification of Cost Function: German Credit Data

Missing Info: Collection of Horse Colic Data

Here is just a list of characteristics; you can pick and examine your traits.

I have listed one dataset for each trait, but you might select 2-3 separate datasets and complete a few small projects to develop your understanding and practice.

For each problem, I would advise you to work systematically from end-to-end, for example, through the following steps in the applied machine learning process:

- Define the question
- Prepare the data
- Assess algorithms
- Improving results
- Write-up of results

It's a vital part of the write-up.

It helps you create a portfolio of projects that you refer back to as a guide for potential projects to get a jump-start and use it as a public curriculum vitae or your growing expertise and capabilities in advanced machine learning.

I don't know about a machine learning platform.

Choose a program or framework (like Weka, R, or scikit-learn) and use this process to learn a tool. Cover both training machine learning and being good at the tool at the same time.

I don't know how to create a computer (or code very well).

Please use Weka. It has a graphical user interface, and no programming is required. I would recommend this to beginners regardless of whether they can program or not since the machine learning process has trouble mapping them too well on the network.

I don't have the time.

With a solid, organized method and a decent tool that encompasses the entire process, I think you can work through a problem in one or two hours. It ensures that you can finish a project in the evening or over two nights.

You pick the amount of detail you want to investigate, and it's a safe thing to keep it light and quick when you're just starting.

I don't have a history in the domain that I model.

The dataset pages give some context to the dataset. You will also dig further by looking at publications or information files following the key dataset.

I have little or no experience going on the challenges of machine learning.

It's time for you to launch. Choose a structured process, choose a basic dataset and a method like Weka, and work on the first problem. Put the first stone in the machine learning base.

I don't have much familiarity with data processing.

There is no requirement for expertise in the data processing. The data set is basic, easy to interpret, and well explained. You just need to read them using the data collection home page and look at the data files themselves.

Real-world examples allow the qualitative definition of machine learning concrete.

You're going on a journey of real-life machine learning challenges. You can see how machine learning can be applied in education, research, technology, and medicine.

Each machine learning issue mentioned also provides a connection to the publicly accessible data collection. It means that you can download the dataset and start training immediately if you are interested in a specific machine learning topic.

Most common datasets for Kaggle

These first ten examples of machine learning challenges have been taken from Kaggle.com's competitive machine learning page. Popularity was based on the number of teams involved.

Team Otto Commodity Recognition Challenge. According to the characteristics of the product info, products are categorized into one of 9 product groups.

Sales of the Rossman Shop. Based on past market data for goods across stores, potential sales are expected.

Bike Sharing Demand. Provided daily bike rental and weather records forecast potential daily bike rental needs.

The Edge in Analytics. Provided the new information of the days, the articles predict which news stories to be famous.

Prediction of Sales Restaurant. Provided the restaurant location's specifics, the restaurant's income in a given year is expected.

Freedom Cooperative Group: Land Inspection Forecast. In consideration of the descriptions of the properties examined, the hazard score for the properties is estimated.

Answer to Springleaf Marketing. Customer attributes predict whether or not they are a marketing priority.

Higgs Boson Learning Machine Challenge. Defined the simulated particle collisions predict whether or not the incident will decay into the Higgs boson.

Forest Cover Prediction Form. Provided the cartographic variables, the forest cover type is expected.

Amazon.com: Employee Access-Challenge. Given the historical improvements in access to services for workers, the resources needed by employees are expected.

Most common databases for study

The next ten machine learning problems are the most common on the University of California's Irvine Machine Learning Repository website, which typically hosts machine learning datasets used by the machine learning research community.

The dataset in Iris. Provided flower measurements in centimeters, the iris species are expected.

Adult datasets. Provided the census results, predicting a person will receive more than $50,000 a year.

Dataset of wine. Due to the chemical study of the wines, the origin of the wind is expected.

Dataset for a care assessment. Information on vehicles forecasts the approximate safety of the vehicle.

Breast Cancer Dataset in Wisconsin. Provided the breast tissue screening examination predicts whether or not the mass is a tumor.

The dataset of Abalone. Provided the dimensions of the Abalone, the age of the Abalone is estimated.

Dataset of Wine Standard. Owing to the different measurements of wine, the consistency of the wine is estimated.

Dataset for heart attack. Given the outcome of different screening examinations, the patient estimates the patient's volume of heart disease.

Dataset of Poker Hand. Provided a database of poker hands, the accuracy of the hand is estimated.

Recognition of human behavior using the dataset of mobile phones. From smartphone movement results, the type of operation conducted by the person carrying the smartphone is expected.

Dataset for forest fires. Due to meteorological and other conditions, the burning area of the forest fires is estimated.

Dataset of Internet Advertising. Provided the descriptions of the photographs on the web pages, predict whether or not the image is advertising.

Normal research datasets can be very obtuse and distant from you and your everyday life. Boring, too. The trick you may like to use is finding and working on a dataset that matters to you.

We'll look at some dataset ideas that you could use to inspire and even speed up your journey to applied machine learning.

Issues of effects

Before that, we looked at the need to focus on topics that have an impact. The challenges that have the most effect are the problems that personally concern you.

There could be topics related to your personal life, interests, or even jobs. Some topics can or may not be resolved right now. The scale and complexity of the dilemma do not matter as long as you are, in any way, involved in the result. The findings are important to you.

For two reasons, this is an effective method:

It permits you to critically approach the problem and apply your logical problem-solving skills to it, which can result in some fascinating outcomes.

Caring about the result is more likely to inspire you to learn new and different approaches, deepen the challenge's definition, and write down your results. Since you think about the result, you're going to make the project more seriously.

There's no old dilemma you can choose. There are a variety of additional considerations:

- **Data:** Machine learning algorithms simulate data problems, and the accuracy of the modeling is usually proportional to the quality of the data. You ought to be able to view and gather data for the sake of the problem.
- **Public:** Can the details and/or the findings be made publicly available? It could be important to you to plan to use the project as part of your machine learning portfolio, which I highly encourage you to do.
- **Issue:** Begin with a question and make sure that an issue needs to be addressed. The query will explain the details that you need to gather and the effect that the result will have on you.

In the next pages, we're going to look at three aspects of your life where you might face issues that you might be able to investigate through machine learning.

Home Machine Learning

Are there challenges and data points in your personal life that you can model using machine learning methods?

Five examples that come to my mind are as follows:

- **Personal Finance:** You should model some of the facets of your personal finance. It may be anything like a weekly spending forecast or a broad purchase forecast. It could even have anything to do with your investment portfolio if that's your business.

- **Transport:** You should model any part of your transportation. It could be the train or bus that you take on your trip on a given day, the journey time, or other detail, such as work arrival time forecast or fuel consumption.
- **Food:** You should model everything about the food you eat. It may be the number, the calories, the snack outlook, or the model of what you expect to buy in a given week.
- **Media:** You should model your media use, such as TV, movies, magazines, music, or websites. An obvious solution will be to model it as a recommendation problem and consider consumption-volume models such as how much you consume when you consume it and any similar trends you might forecast.
- **Fitness:** You might be able to model any part of personal fitness. It may be weight, BMI, body measurement, or an element of stamina, such as the number of sit-ups or the time to complete the workout. How about modeling whether or not you're going to the gym for a given day (what will the inputs be?).

Know, you need to get access to data, which is very likely to mean that you have to spend some time calculating and gathering data.

Learning Computer for a Hobby

Have you got a hobby other than machine learning? Think about what data you would be able to obtain from a model specific to your hobby.

Five types of hobbies that you can or may want to emulate include:

- **Sports:** You can model a team or league results. You may be part of fantasy sports teams, and you may be involved in modeling individual athletes' success. There is also a casino side to sporting results that could ignite your curiosity (be careful). You might have a child or family member who plays a sport for weeks that may be a little more related to you with a problem and a data source.
- **Games:** You can model a part of the game you're playing. It can be a board game, a card game, or a video game. You may simulate and forecast win/loss outcomes, particular result ratings, or specific game moves.
- **Arts and crafts:** You may be an amateur artist or craftsman and upload your pictures to your creations' public social photo album. You could model and forecast whether the photo you upload is of interest to third parties or not (in the form of views or comments). A similar methodology may be used in-person for control groups (family members?) and with many other art types that could involve a subjective evaluation of interest or quality.

- **Language:** You could model any part of the language that you or a friend or family member are learning. If flashcards are used, you might get into the fascinating problem of modeling whether a given card's contents would be remembered. Other facets of language acquisition, such as the rate of new works learned and the level of mistakes, may also be modeled. Collecting data can be a fascinating challenge.
- **Photograph:** You may be a bird watcher, a nature enthusiast, or have some other excuse to photograph nature with all its diversity. You could model the issue of classifying the leaves/birds/animals' images in their categories. You may also model the issue of whether the photo in question contains an object of interest, such as your family dog or your face.

Gravitate towards hobbies that have datasets that you can conveniently rely on and model.

Learning Robots at Work

Will you have access to data at work or stuff you're working on? It might be your blog or something else online, or it might be detailed or connected to something that your job produces or publishes.

Visitors: Would you model a visit to your website. Perhaps a visitor's demographic attribute, such as a forum, browser, etc., or perhaps a visitor's source or the number of page views over a span based on content shared.

Customers: Like guests, are the consumer assets that can be modeled? It can include sales amounts, shopping cart items, purchase times, or related demographic statistics. I like this environment because it can shed a lot of new information (data support) about a company that was taken for granted.

Conversion: Can their conversion efficiency be modeled? There may be factors of conversion, such as time or profiles of the consumer. It could be the forecast of conversion chains, such as a trial, charged, up-selling.

Churn: In the service sector, churn is something that is critical and is now being modeled. Is there any sort of turnover that isn't being modeled? Churn from the experiments, maybe. Churn from email lists or RSS subscriptions?

Proprietary records are any special or fascinating data that your company produces or has access to. What questions should you pose about the data that could be worth modeling? For example, meteorological data, output data, mining data, etc.

Be aware of privacy and data ownership issues. Before viewing the details, you may need permission to keep the findings private or internal to your organization.

3.1: Build a Machine Learning Portfolio

Designers and artists usually use a portfolio to present samples of recent work to potential customers and employers.

Craft, painting, and photography are examples where the work result is imaginative and empiric, were asking others what you should do is not the same as showing them.

I'm trying to persuade you that creating a machine learning portfolio has a benefit for you, others, and the community.

You'll find out just what the machine learning portfolio is, the kinds of projects that can be used, and how to make your portfolio fit for you.

Benefits of a Machine Learning Portfolio Whether you're just starting as a novice of machine learning or a seasoned veteran, a machine learning portfolio will keep you on track and show your skills. Creating a portfolio in machine learning is a beneficial practice for you and others.

Benefits to You

Built-up a list of completed machine learning applications will keep you focused, inspired and leverage future projects.

Focus: Each project has a well-defined goal and endpoint. Small ventures, limited in effort and money, will keep the pace high.

Information Base: The corpus of finished projects offers a knowledge base for you to draw on and exploit as you drive projects farther away from the comfort zone.

Trajectory: There are so many shiny items to investigate, telling yourself that you're searching for consistent collection projects that can be used as a lever to keep you on track.

Benefits among Others

Others may use the portfolio of finished tasks to measure unique qualifications, leadership skills and drive demonstration.

Skills: A project will show your skills concerning a particular problem area, method, library technology stack, or algorithm.

Communication: The project must be known, at least in terms of its intent and its conclusions. Curing a successful portfolio requires outstanding leadership abilities that tautologically show the ability to interact well with professional subjects.

Motivation: Focusing on and completing side tasks, regardless of the scale of the scope, requires a certain degree of self-discipline. The fact that you have managed to build up a portfolio is a monument to your interest in the subject and the ability to control your time.

Benefits for the Society

Sharing the projects in public adds benefits to the entire machine learning ecosystem.

Commitment: A public initiative will receive input from third parties and include enhancements and changes that both you and the group can benefit from.

Starting point: A public portfolio project may offer a starting point from which others can learn and expand on, maybe with their small project or something serious.

Case Example: a public initiative may provide a study point for a special or fascinating algorithm activity or problem decomposition, the very root of innovation.

Luckily, I've persuaded you that developing a portfolio in machine learning has certain benefits that concern you. First, we'll look at just what a portfolio in machine learning is.

Create a portfolio in machine learning

A portfolio of machine learning is a series of finished individual programs, each of which uses machine learning somehow. The folio provides a list of projects which allows for the analysis of particular projects.

Five attributes of an efficient machine learning portfolio include:

- **Available:** I support making the portfolio available in the form of a freely accessible website or a set of public code repositories. You want people to find, read, blog, and, if possible, use your work.
- **Small:** Each project should be small in scale in terms of ambition, money, and, most importantly, time (10-20 hours). You're busy, and it's hard to keep your attention on it. See the methodology for my Small Projects.

- **Completion:** Small projects help you complete your projects. Set and accomplish a modest project goal. Like mini-experiments, you show the results of your achievements and weaknesses, which are all valuable lessons.
- **Independent:** Each project should be independent to be understood in isolation. It doesn't mean that you can't exploit past work; it means that the idea makes sense on its own as a stand-alone piece of work.
- **Understandable:** each project must express its intent and results accurately and efficiently (at the very least). Spend some time to make sure a fresh pair of eyes knows what you've done and why it's important.

Four types of small project ideas that could inspire you to include:

- Investigate the properties of a machine learning platform or library.
- Study the actions of a machine learning algorithm.
- Investigate and characterize a data set or machine learning problem.
- Implement a machine learning algorithm in your chosen programming language.

Many of the proposals for projects that you didn't consider were portfolio pieces include:

The course's job: Your simple presentation of your notes and homework for your machine learning tutorial (such as a MOOC).

Book Review: The straightforward presentation of your reading notes and your review of the machine learning book.

Software Review: The simple presentation and working samples for using a machine learning software tool or library.

Competition Participation: Notes and outcomes for participation in a machine learning competition, such as Kaggle, are specifically presented.

Comment: An article in response to a machine learning-themed blog post or a detailed answer to a machine learning relevant question on a Q&A forum such as Quora, Reddit Machine Learning, or Cross Validated.

Now that you know what a machine learning portfolio is and have some suggestions about ventures, let's look at how to transform your portfolio into an amazing one.

Making your portfolio high

You need to do some light ads to make your portfolio shine. Don't worry, and it's none of that slimy stuff; it's just a good old-fashioned thing to get the message out.

Repository Code

Try using a shared source code website, such as GitHub or BitBucket, which naturally lists the public ventures. These sites allow you to include a readme file in the root of and project that explains what the project is all about. Use this function to explain the intent and findings of each project explicitly. Don't be afraid to add photos, graphics, videos, and links.

Provide simple guidelines for downloading the project and re-creating the results (if there is code or experimentation involved). You want people to get the job done again, make it as quick as possible (i.e., type this to download, then type this to build and run it).

Projects curate

You can hit any old GitHub project together, but only include your best, clearest, most interesting work in your machine learning portfolio.

Please curate your projects like a gallery. Choose the ones that best show your talents, desires, and ability. Show off what you can do and what you've done. Sees ideas of self-promotion will feedback to ventures that you may like to pursue. Be clear about your vision, where you want to be, and what projects you want to tackle that will help you get there. It's its process.

Current Findings

Spend a lot of time writing the results. Explain how they contribute to the goals of the project. Explain the effect they have or may have had on the domain. List the possibilities for extensions that you might or would like to pursue if you had another month or year to delve deeper into the idea.

Build tables, graphics, and some other fun pictures that will help you share your story. Writing down your observations as a blog post. Make a brief screenshot of how you got the results and a tiny PowerPoint presentation of what it entails, put it on YouTube for bonus points. It can be inserted into your blog post and connected to a readme file from your project repository.

Based on the results you have and how important they are to you (such as doing well at the Kaggle competition), you might try making a technical report and uploading it to Scribd, and uploading SlideShare slides.

Promoting the job

You will share the specifics of each project when you complete it. You could be doing one a week based on the number of free hours you may find in your research and/or job environment. Sharing social media ties is a good start, like Twitter, Facebook, and Google+.

I will encourage you to add each project (or only your best projects) to LinkedIn as "projects." It promotes ventures' notion, and you will need to build a work for them to be identified against. Suggest the name of your blog, your single trading firm, or concoct a relevant work and title such as "Machine Learning Supremacy" (Wink) or "Self Education."

Now that we have some suggestions about making our portfolio shine and getting the message out, we should look at some examples of machine learning portfolios.

The trend in the Portfolio of Machine Learning

The notion of a code portfolio isn't new, and it's been baked into GitHub. What is noteworthy is that, in recent interviews with data scientists and administrators, portfolios are asked, along with participation in machine learning competitions and completion of online preparation.

Like the demo code in programming interviews, Machine Learning portfolios are becoming a serious part of recruiting.

Look for examples of good (or at least completed) machine learning portfolios. Look for people doing well in machine learning contests, and they generally have a wonderful set of projects listed in their blogs and their public code repositories.

Look for developers to open-source machine learning projects, and they will have incredible videos, apps, and program extensions on their websites and public code repositories.

3.2: Get Paid to Apply Machine Learning

Would you want to do machine learning and get paid for it? Be selective of what you desire. I describe a blueprint that you should use to learn enough machine learning to help small companies and startups fulfill their general data needs. It's not easy, and you're going to have to work hard in your comfort zone. You're going to have to talk to real people in the real world!

Blueprint

The blueprint provided in this post will take you from a passionate interest in machine learning and commitment to learning through to being willing and confident to work through general data challenges in small and medium-sized businesses or startups to have a solution.

The blueprint for the route is as follows:

- Establish a base for you
- Build your portfolio
- Delivery of options

You should adapt the guide to your needs, provided your context and interests.

To be sure, we're just interested in advanced machine learning. We're only interested in theories and tools as long as they help you to understand your challenge better and produce better outcomes on the topic you're working on.

It's a counter-intuitive but rather positive perspective. Learn what you need in time and concentrate on achieving outcomes. It's about getting good outcomes, not excellence, consistently.

Set up a base.

You need to learn enough applied machine learning to have faith to work from start to finish. Define it specifically and produce the model or report needed as a project result.

Choose and understand the procedure. Study a step-by-step method that you will pursue that will carry you from problem creation to outcome execution. Examples include KDD, Crisp-DM, OSEMN, and others.

Pick a tool and master it. Learn the tool or repositories you can use to complete your chosen process. I suggest one of Weka, sci-kit-learn, R, based on your interests and preferences.

Train small databases. Download the tiny datasets you can work on. Spend a lot of time with the UCI ML repository.

You're ready to move on when you're secure and competent enough to pick up an arbitrary in-memory issue and use the instrument to work from start to finish.

Create a portfolio

If you have a foundation's ability to deal with challenges, you need reliable metrics that others will use to assess your capabilities. You need finished tasks to show your ability to execute.

You will do so by creating a portfolio of completed machine learning projects.

Interlude of Mentality

Pause for a moment to think about a boss or small business owner with a data concern.

As such, you recruit programmers depending on their ability to produce project results to other organizations and open source. You recruit advertisers based on their ability to boost conversions to attack the bottom line. If such a boss wanted a "data person" to deliver a report or a model, what would they do to determine whether a candidate could deliver a result?

I would like to see proof of finished projects in that position. Other than that, I'd like to see proof of finished projects that are close to the outcome I'm searching for.

Your portfolio of businesses

Choose a theme. It is the sort of project you want to focus on. No-brainer will be consumer data records (high-value customers, predictions of prospects that convert, etc.).

Find free datasets for you. You need to find the datasets that you can use to be similar to or on your theme. Look at rivalry websites like Kaggle and Cup as a starting point. There are a lot of public access datasets you can practice on these days!

Completion of programs. Treat each dataset as a customer project and add the method to it to produce the result. It enables you to assume the client's position and make an informed guess about the result they are hoping for (model or report on a specific question, etc.)

Write-up. Write up the results as a semi-formal job product and host it publicly online.

This last point is the key, and I'm going to elaborate on it.

Ideally, make each part of the process scripted so that you can re-run at any time you encounter glitches or gain insight. Try adding all the programming and scripts to the project's public GitHub account.

Write the outcome of each project as a technical paper or PowerPoint. Consider taking a brief video of your observations. Host a GitHub article, a blog, or something. Write the project to your public LinkedIn profile.

Your goal is to have a position where you can point someone to see all the projects you've completed at a glance, then dig into one and see what you've done and what you've created.

You're happy to move on until you can logically persuade someone that you're capable of achieving success on your theme. I think the small scale of 3-5 finished projects would be fair.

Providing Solutions

Now that you have the potential to perform and show it, it's time for you to complete ventures in the wild.

You're going to have to go out there and talk to the public. This move is going to be a fantastic filter. This move can be a little frightening and a little complicated, and it's going to be your real test.

Find someone you can help out with. Please use your social network. Take part in groups, have introductions, etc. Look for a small business or startup that you can meet face to face (ideally) and find out about their challenges and get access to their info.

Be frank with me. Say the reality on that. Explain where you came from, what you did, and what you should do. Try doing the first free or inexpensive piece of work to get your first project under your belt. Your direction is an asset, indicating that you are hungry, willing to produce, and motivated. We all want to collaborate with people who are posing this way.

Deliver it. Do the job. Specify the project, keep the scale minimal and transparent, and deliver what you think you can deliver. Again, don't guarantee something you haven't done before or don't know how to do it.

Repeat.

Keep tasks minimal and short in duration. Ideally, produce within 1-2 weeks. You need energy, good results, and quick learning for your customer.

3.3: Machine Learning for Money

You can work using your machine learning expertise as a machine learning programmer, data analyst, or data scientist. That's the target of a lot of people who are in touch with me.

There are other choices, too. I want to show some of the other choices and try to turn the gears around.

There are many possibilities; with a large amount of data available, you just need to think about and discover some valuable queries. These are the issues that individuals and companies will have to address.

Impact – First

Let's start with some methods before we plunge into an example domain.

Like every other machine learning query, you are pursuing the machine learning process, but you choose a domain and ask if there is a demand to get the question addressed.

Start a query in a domain (define your problem well). Choose a query depending on the influence it has on the domain. In this scenario, the effect could be a return. Play thought exercises with an idealized paradigm that could make perfect predictions.

Collect the data you need to answer the query (data selection).

Clean and plan the data to make it appropriate for modeling (data preparation)

Spot the algorithms to search the problem. Be sure to begin with, the easiest possible models and use them as a starting point.

Tune the most effective models and use strategies such as thresholds and sets to get the most out of the models you have picked (improve results).

Show the findings or bring the machine into action and set up close watches (present results).

Ideally, the more specifically you answer the issue, the greater the return (or, the bigger the bets you can make).

Your startup

If you have your own company or web startup, so you can take a close look at the data you are currently gathering. It is not unprecedented for various data collection applications to be hosted on a web startup, such as Kiss Metrics, Google Analytics, and many others. How will this data be used to impact the bottom line?

In my opinion, this is more data analyst work than machine learning work, but you can still bust a regression model to see if it gives more lift than a basic quintile model.

In the previous post, we discussed this a bit. However, here are some suggestions of places that you may want to look at:

- **Customer conversions:** Model the characteristics of consumers that are migrating or not converting.
- **P-sell and cross-sell:** model the features of consumers that give up-sell or cross-sell conversion.
- **Acquisition Strategies:** model the importance of consumers, buy their acquisition strategies.
- **Retention Strategies:** Model the ROI approach for the retention of consumers.
- **Customer Churn:** Model the characteristics of consumers that are churn or not churn.

Begin with the effect on the bottom line and move backward to the questions you need to ask to make a decision. Once you can answer the query and make a forecast about a potential client, spend time developing and evaluating action techniques that you can use to affect or build on the prediction.

Development

You may be a developer or programmer who knows how to code, build and release applications. Think of useful online questions that you would be able to answer using machine learning techniques.

Are there any suggestions or guidelines that you can make that are valuable?

Any of the off-the-cuff explanations that come to mind are several publicly accessible social media data:

- **Kick Starter:** Model the characteristics of a successful or unsuccessful kick start campaign.
- **Social Media Profile:** Model the characteristics of a good social media profile (visits or page ranking) on LinkedIn, Google+, or Facebook.
- **Social News:** Model the functionality of a good post on a social news platform like Hacker News or Reddit.
- **Sales Page:** Model the functionality of a popular product sales page for e-commerce or information items.

Making money out of insights into social media data is a cramped room. If you want to take this idea seriously, you're going to have to be pretty creative with the features you're using to model the problem. The engineering function would be your contribution, even more than the individual models.

This strategy would most likely involve the compilation and processing of complicated datasets. Some datasets are not a neat matrix of functions. The modeling method will define the desired result first, determine its predictive power, and then make the forecasts that you give to clients.

Finance and Gaming

Finance and gaming are the clear choices for making money from machine learning. I am hesitant to recommend these places. They might very definitely be dangerous sirens, I suppose. Like Venus flytraps, they draw and eat programmers and machine-learning practitioners.

The advantage is that the decisions are very straightforward (which horse will win or which stock to buy/sell), and you can deploy your own money behind the decisions. I would say that modeling issues that are easy for you to grasp, certain financial instruments can be very complicated.

I had my toe in high-frequency trading and portfolio optimization. It could be frightening stuff but exciting. I've been suggesting paper-trading for a while, and there are fantastic APIs that you can use for your data source. Please see How to make $500k with computer learning and HFT (high-frequency trading) and Machine Learning Financial Software. You may want to take a look at it, too.

Quantopian

I haven't tested any gambling questions, but I've seen some of the approaches I plan to find in the literature, such as ranking scales. Think horse and dog races, sports betting (2 player games), and casino games like poker.

Race yourself. Focus on the problem, gather the data, and easily identify some of the baseline outcomes. Your goal is to build on your own best performance and exploit each that can help. Your goal is not to outperform domain experts, at least for a long time.

Competitions

You can make money by taking part in machine learning competitions. My recommendation is that cash prizes are not the main reason for competition participation. You will make a lot of money by seeking customers to meet directly. However, top athletes will win cash prizes.

Many of the areas you can find at machine learning competitions include:

- The Challenge of Kaggle.gov
- Innocent Tuned

Competitions will be a perfect way to practice, test, and develop your abilities. Usually, there is a lot of knowledge exchange on these pages, and you will find out, and algorithms and resources are hot.

Machine Learning

Chapter 4: Applied Machine Learning Process

The first step in every project is to identify your dilemma. You can use the most efficient and shiniest algorithms around, but the conclusions would be useless if you solve the wrong problem.

In this part, you will learn how to think thoroughly about your problem before you get started. It is probably the most critical part of the implementation of machine learning.

Issue definition of the structure

I use a basic paradigm to describe a new issue with machine learning. The system allows me to understand the elements and inspiration behind the dilemma quickly and whether machine learning is acceptable or not.

The process includes reacting to three questions with differing degrees of thoroughness:

- Step 1: What's the Problem?
- Step 2: Why is there a need to solve the problem?
- Step 3: How am I going to solve the problem?

Step 1: What's the problem

The first step is to identify the problem. I'm using a variety of techniques to gather this information.

Definition of the informal

Describe the dilemma as if you were explaining it to a friend or colleague. It will offer a perfect starting point for outlining places that you might like to fill in. It also provides the basis for a summary of one sentence you can use to share your interpretation of the issue.

E.g., I need software that tells me which tweets are going to get retweets.

Formalism:

In the previous chapter describing machine learning, you've heard about Tom Mitchell's machine learning formalism. It's here to refresh your mind again.

A computer program is said to benefit from experience E in any class of tasks T and performance evaluation P if its performance in tasks T, as calculated by P, increases with experience E.

Using this formalism to describe the problems of T, P, and E.

For instance:

Task (T): Identify a tweet that has not been released to get retweets or not.

Experience (E): a corpus of tweets for an account where others have retweeted and some may not.

Performance (P): Precision of grouping, the number of tweets correctly predicted from all tweets taken as a percentage.

Assumptions:

Build a list of observations and phrases about the issue. These could be thumb rules and domain-specific knowledge that you believe can get you to a feasible solution quicker.

It can help illustrate problems that can be checked against actual evidence, and breakthroughs and progress emerge as theories and best practices are found to be false in the face of real data. It may also help illustrate aspects of the problem specification that may need to be challenged, relaxed, or tightened.

For instance:

- The particular terms used on the model in the tweet matter.
- The person who retweets does not matter to the model.
- The number of retweets may be of interest to the model.
- Older tweets are less predictive than more recent tweets.

Related concerns

What other challenges have you encountered or may you conceive about as the dilemma you're trying to solve? Other issues may remind you of the problem you are trying to solve by highlighting limitations in your phrase of the problem, such as time dimensions and logical drift (where the concept being modeled changes over time). Other issues can also point to algorithms and data transformations that may be used to detect performance tests.

For example, the related issue will be e-mail spam discrimination that uses text messages as input data and requires binary classification decisions.

Stage 2: Why does the dilemma need to be resolved?

The second step is to think critically about whether you want or need to fix the dilemma.

Motivation:

Consider your inspiration to solve the dilemma. What needs will be met until the spot is resolved?

E.g., you could solve the problem as a learning activity. It is helpful to explain as you may determine that you do not want to use the most effective approach to tackle the dilemma but may wish to try systems that you are not familiar with to learn new techniques.

Alternatively, you can need to fix the dilemma as part of your work duties, essentially to retain your career.

Benefits of Solution

Value the advantages of getting the dilemma fixed. What are the skills that make it possible?

It is essential to be transparent about the advantages of the issue being discussed to ensure that you capitalize on it. These incentives may be used to market the project to peers and administrators to purchase extra time or budget money.

If it affects you directly, be sure what those benefits are and how you'll know where you've got them. E.g., if it's a tool or resource, what are you going to be able to do with that utility that you can't do now, and why is that meaningful to you?

Usage of Solution

Think about how the solution to the dilemma can be used and what kind of life you imagine the answer to be. As programmers, we always assume the job is finished as soon as the software is written, but the actual project is only starting its maintenance life.

How the solution will be used will affect the design and criteria of the solution that you implement.

Think if you want to write a paper to show the findings or whether you want to make the solution workable. When you want to run a solution, understand the functional and non-functional specifications you have for an answer, much like a software project.

Step 3: How am I going to solve the problem?

In this third and final step in identifying the problem, discover how you can manually solve it.

List what data you would gather step-by-step, how you would plan it, and how you would develop a program to solve the problem. It could involve prototypes and tests that you will like to conduct that are a gold mine since they would illustrate concerns and doubts in the domain that may be investigated.

It's a good weapon. It will illustrate problems that can potentially be addressed satisfactorily using a manually applied solution. It also collects valuable domain information that has been trapped so far as to where the data is currently stored, what kind of functionality might be useful and several other info.

Collect all of these details as they appear, and amend the last parts of the problem description. The assumptions and laws of thumb in particular.

4.1: Prepare Your Data

Machine learning algorithms are used to learn from results. You must send them the correct data to solve the problem you want to solve.

Even if you have useful info, you need to make sure that it is in an available size, format, and even meaningful functionality.

You'll learn how to plan data for a machine learning algorithm. It is a huge problem, and you're trying to cover the basics.

Stages of Data Processing

The more disciplined you manage your records, the more reliable and better outcomes you are likely to produce. The method for preparing data for a machine learning algorithm can be outlined in three steps:

Stages 1: Select Data

Stage 2: Pre-process details

Stages 3: Convert the data

You can follow this method linearly, but it is more likely to be iterative with many loops.

Stages 1: Select Data

This move concerns the specification of the subset of all available data that you will be dealing with. There is still a great need to include all the available evidence that the "more is better" principle would hold. It may or may not be valid.

You need to consider what evidence you need to answer the query or topic you're working on. Make any assumptions about the data you need, and be sure to note those assumptions to verify them later, if necessary.

Here are some questions that will help you think about this process:

What is the sum of data that you have available? E.g., time, database tables, connected systems. Ensure that you have a good picture of everything you can need.

What data is not available that you would like to make public? E.g., data that is not or cannot be registered. You may be able to extract or simulate this data.

What kind of data do you not require to fix the problem? It is almost often better to remove data than to add data. Notice which details you have omitted and why.

It is only in minor challenges, such as competitiveness or toy datasets, where the data has already been chosen for you.

Stage 2: Pre-process details

Once you have chosen the data, you need to know how to use the data. This pre-processing phase is about placing the desired data in a form that you can use.

Three standard measures for pre-processing data are formatting, cleaning, and sampling:

- **Formatting:** The data you chose may not be in a format appropriate for you to work with. The data may be in a relational database, and you would prefer it to be in a flat disc, or the data may be in a proprietary file format, and you would like it to be in a relational database or a text file.
- **Cleaning**: Cleaning data is the replacement or correction of lost data. There may be missing data instances, and do not include the data you think you need to fix. These instances will need to be deleted. Also, specific attributes may contain confidential information, and these attributes may need to be anonymized or deleted from the data.
- **Sampling:** There might be much more data available than you need to deal with. More data can result in much longer running times for algorithms and higher computational and memory requirements. You may take a smaller representative sample of the selected data, which could be much quicker for investigating and prototyping solutions, before considering the whole dataset.

The machine learning tools you use on the data will likely influence the pre-processing you will be required to perform. You're likely to revisit this step.

Stages 3: Turn the data

The final step is to convert the data for the operation. The particular algorithm you are dealing with and the understanding of the problem domain will affect this step. You will most definitely have to review the various transformations of the pre-processed data while focusing on your problem.

Three common data transformations are scaling, decomposition attributes, and aggregation attributes. This stage is often referred to as the engineering of functionality.

- **Scaling:** Pre-processed data which include attributes with a mixture of scales for different amounts, such as dollars, kilograms, and volume of sales. Many machine learning techniques, such as data attributes, have the same scale as 0 to 1 for the smallest and largest value for a given function. Consider any scaling functions you might need to perform.
- **Decomposition:** There may be elements that reflect a complex idea that may be more useful for machine learning when separated into components. An example is a date that may have day and time components that could be further divided. Perhaps only the hour of the day is relevant to the problem being resolved. Consider what kind of decompositions you can perform.
- **Aggregation:** There may be features that can be aggregated into a single part that would be more meaningful to the problem you're trying to solve. For example, each time a customer logs into a system, there may be data instances that could be aggregated into a count for the number of logins that would allow the additional samples to be discarded. Consider what type of aggregation would be able to perform.

Identify Outliers in the Results

Many machine learning algorithms are adaptive to the range and distribution of the input data attribute values.

Outliers in input data will distort and deceive machine learning algorithms' training process, resulting in longer training times, less reliable models, and consequently worse outcomes.

Well before training data predictive models are prepared, outliers can lead to misleading representations and, in turn, misleading interpretations of the data obtained. Outliers can skew the summary distribution of attribute values in descriptive statistics such as mean and standard deviation and plots such as histograms and scatterplots, compressing the data body.

Finally, outliers can include examples of data instances that are important to the problem, such as anomalies in fraud detection and computer protection.

Outline Simulation

Outliers are unusual beliefs that fall a long way apart from the other findings. For example, outliers may be values on the tails of the distribution in regular distribution.

The outlier recognition method has many names in data mining and machine learning, such as outlier mining, outlier simulation, novelty detection, and anomaly detection.

A useful taxonomy of external detection techniques, as follows:

Extreme Value Analysis: Assess the mathematical tails of the underlying data distribution. E.g., statistical methods such as z-scores for univariate results.

Probabilistic and Predictive Models: Assess unexpected instances of a probabilistic data model. For example, Gaussian mixture models optimized using expectations-maximization.

Linear Models: projection methods that model data in lower dimensions using linear correlations. For example, the critical component analysis and data with significant residual errors may be outliers.

Proximity-based Models: Data instances that are separated from the mass of the data as determined by cluster, density, or nearest neighbor analysis.

Information-Theoretic Models: Outliers are detected as data instances that increase the dataset's complexity (minimum length of code).

High-Dimensional Outlier Detection: methods that scan subspaces for outliers offer a breakdown of distance-dependent measurements in higher dimensions (the curse of dimensionality).

The interpretability of the outlier model is of crucial significance. Background or justification is needed to decide whether a single data instance is or is not an outlier.

In his chapter on Data Mining and Information Discovery Handbook, Irad Ben-Gal suggests a taxonomy of outlier models as univariate or multivariate and parametric and nonparametric. It is a helpful way to organize approaches based on what we know about the results. For instance:

- Are you found to have outliers of one or more attributes (univariate or multivariate methods)?

- May you presume a statistical distribution from which observations have been sampled or not (parametric or nonparametric)?

Getting Underway

There are many approaches and a lot of research being conducted to spot outsiders. Start by making certain assumptions and design tests to detect the results of these assumptions against a metric of efficiency or accuracy.

I propose going in a step-by-step approach of extreme value analysis, proximity methods, and prediction methods.

Study of Extreme Worth

You do not need to know sophisticated statistical techniques to search, interpret and sort out the results. Start with intense value analysis.

Emphasis on the methods of univariate

Display data utilizing scatterplots, histograms, and boxes, and scan for severe values

Assume a distribution (Gaussian) and search for values greater than 2 or 3 standard deviations from the mean or 1.5 times from the first or third quartile.

Fill out the training dataset candidate outliers and test the efficiency of your models.

Methods of proximity

Once you've explored simplified extreme value approaches, consider switching to proximity-based methods.

Using clustering approaches to classify the natural clusters of the data (such as the k-means algorithm)

Identify and mark the centroid cluster.

Identify data instances that are within a fixed distance or percentage distance from cluster centroids.

Fill out the training dataset candidate outliers and test the efficiency of your models.

Methods of projection

Projection techniques are relatively easy to implement and easily illustrate extraneous values.

Using projection tools to summaries the data in two dimensions (e.g., PCA, SOM, or Sammon mapping)

View mapping and classify outliers by hand

Use the proximity measurements of predicted values or codebook vectors to classify outliers.

Fill out the training dataset candidate outliers and test the efficiency of your models.

High Methods to Outliers

The preferred approach is to shift towards models that are resilient to outliers. There are robust regression models that minimize the median least square error rather than the mean (so-called robust regression) but are more computationally intensive. There are also processes, such as decision trees, that are resistant to outliers.

Boost Model Pre-Processing Accuracy

Before you model your dilemma, you must pre-process your raw data. Specific planning can depend on the data you have available and the machine learning algorithms you choose to use.

Pre-processing of data can also lead to unforeseen changes in the quality of the model. It may be because the relationship in the data has been simplified or blurred.

Data planning is a crucial step, and you can play with data pre-processing measures suitable for your data to see how you can achieve the desired increase in model accuracy.

There are three forms of pre-processing that you may consider for your data:

- Add attributes to the data.
- Delete attributes from data
- Turn the characteristics of your data.

Add Data Attributes to

Advanced models can derive relationships from complex attributes, but some models need these relationships to be spelled out explicitly. Deriving new details from your training data to be used in the modeling process will give you a boost in model efficiency.

Dummy Attributes: The categorical attributes can be transformed to n-binary points, where n is the number of divisions (or levels) the fact has. Such DE standardized or decomposed facts are known as dummy attributes or dummy variables.

Transformed Attribute: A changed variation of the attribute may be applied to the dataset to allow a linear approach to manipulate possible linear and nonlinear relationships between facts. Easy transformations such as log, square and square root can be used.

Missing Data: Attributes of missing data which have missing data imputed using a useful tool, such as k-nearest neighbors.

Delete attributes of data

Some methods do not perform well for redundant or duplicate attributes. You can improve the consistency of the model by deleting characteristics from the results.

Projection: Training data can be projected onto lower-dimensional spaces, but it still characterizes the data's interaction. A common technique is the Principal Component Analysis (PCA), where the critical tools key components can be used as a reduced collection of input attributes.

Spatial Symbol: The spatial sign projection of the data transforms the data on a multidimensional sphere's surface. The findings can illustrate the presence of outliers that can be changed or omitted from the data.

Correlation Attributes: Any algorithms decline in value due to the presence of strongly correlated attributes. Pairwise attributes with high correlations can be detected, and most correlated details can be excluded from the data.

Turn the characteristics of data.

The transformation of training data will minimize the skewness of data and the importance of outliers in the data. Many models expect the data to be transformed before you can use the algorithm.

Centering: Transform the data so that it has a mean of zero and a standard deviation of one. It is commonly referred to as data standardization.

Scaling: The standard transformation of scaling is to map data from the original scale to a scale between zero and one. It is commonly referred to as data normalization.

Delete Skew: Skew data is data that has a distribution that is moved to one side or the other (larger or smaller) rather than usually distributed. Some techniques presume that the information is naturally distributed and will do better if the skew is eliminated. Please consider replacing the variable with the log, square root, or the reciprocal of the values.

Box-Cox: A Transform Box-Cox or a transformer family should be used to change the data to minimize the skew accurately.

Binning: Numeric data can be made discreet by sorting values into bins. It is generally called discretization of data. This method can be done manually, but it is more efficient if carried out routinely and automatically using a heuristic that makes sense in the domain.

Discover Feature Engineering, How to Engineer Features, and How to Get Nice

If your goal is to achieve the best possible outcomes from a statistical model, you need to get the most out of what you've got. It means getting the best results from the algorithms you're using. It also requires making the best out of the data to work with the algorithms.

How do you get the best out of your predictive modeling data?

It is the issue that the method and experience of feature engineering can overcome.

The performance of all Machine Learning algorithms depends on how you show the results.

Function Engineering Significance

Your data attributes can directly affect the statistical models you use and the outcomes you will obtain.

You may say that: the more features you plan and select, the better the outcomes you can produce. It is real, but it is also deceptive.

The outcomes you produce are the format you use, the data you have available, and the prepared features. Also, the frame of the issue and the quantitative metrics you use to estimate accuracy play a role. Your findings rely on a variety of interdependent properties.

You need great features that explain the structure of your results.

Great features mean greater versatility.

You can pick "the wrong models" (less than optimal) and still get a decent outcome. Many models can pick up on a robust data structure. The simplicity of useful features would encourage you to use less complicated versions that are simpler to run, easier to grasp, and easier to manage. It is a desirable thing.

Better features mean more comfortable models.

With well-designed features, you can select "wrong parameters" (less than optimal) and still get good results for the same purposes. You don't have to try as hard to choose the best templates and the most optimized parameters.

With useful functionality, you are closer to the underlying problem and represent all the data you have available. You will use it to describe the underlying problem better.

What's Feature Engineering?

Here's how I describe the engineering feature:

Feature engineering is the method of converting raw data into features that best reflect the underlying predictive modeling issue, resulting in increased model accuracy of unknown data.

In this description, you can see the dependencies:

- The success metrics that you have selected (RMSE? AUC?)
- The structure of the problem (classification? regression?)
- Predictive templates that you use (SVM?)
- The raw data that you selected and prepared (samples? formatting? cleaning?)

Feature Engineering is a matter of representation.

Machine learning algorithms learn from sample data to solve a query.

In this sense, function engineering asks: what is the best representation of the sample data to find a solution to your problem?

It's intense. Doing well in machine learning and in artificial intelligence usually falls to the issue of representation. It's challenging, maybe unknowable (or at best intractable), to know the best term to use, a priori.

You need to transform the inputs into stuff that the algorithm can comprehend.

Function: Feature Technology is the Craft of

It's an art as architecture is art, as scripting is art, as medicine is art.

There are well-defined methods that are methodological, proven, and known.

The data is a variable, and it's different every time. You're good at choosing which techniques to use and when by experience. Empirical apprenticeship. Like engineering, like programming, like medicine, like machine learning generally.

Sub-The challenges of Function Engineering

It's normal to think about feature engineering as one thing.

E.g., feature engineering was a feature construction for me for a long time.

I'd say to myself, "I'm doing function engineering right now," and I'd like to wonder, "How do I break down or aggregate raw data to help explain the underlying problem?" The goal was right, but the methodology was one of many.

In this section, we look at these several methods and the particular sub-problems they plan to solve. Everyone may be an in-depth article of its own, as they are broad and significant fields of practice and analysis.

Feature: A valuable attribute for your job of modeling

Let's start with the data and what the function is.

Tabular data is defined in terms of observations or instances (rows) consisting of variables or attributes (columns). A fact might be a function.

The definition of a function, which is separate from the attribute, makes more sense in the context of a problem. Apart is an element that can be helpful or meaningful to your question. It is an essential aspect of the observation to think about the structure of the problem that is being modeled.

I use the word "meaningful" to discriminate attributes from functions. Some of them may not. I don't think there's anything like a non-meaningful function. If a position does not affect the situation, it is not part of the issue.

An image is an observation in computer vision, but an attribute may be a line in the picture. In natural language processing, a text or tweet may be an observation, and a phrase or word count may be a feature. In speech recognition, an expression may be an observation, but an attribute may be a single word or a phoneme.

Feature Importance: an assessment of the utility of a product

You will independently measure the utility of the functions.

It can be useful as a precursor for choosing features. Features are given points which their ratings can then rank. The parts with the highest scores will be selected for inclusion in the training dataset, while the remaining scores can be skipped.

Feature value scores will also provide you with the knowledge you can use to remove or create new features that are identical but distinct from those considered useful.

A function may be significant if it is strongly correlated to the dependent variable (the thing being predicted). Coefficients of association and other univariate (each parameter is treated independently) are standard approaches.

More sophisticated predictive modeling algorithms execute features of significance and selection internally when building their model. Examples include MARS, Random Forest, and Gradient Boosted Machinery. These models will also report on the variable importance found during the model preparation process.

Function Extraction: Automated building of new features from raw data

Any results are much too voluminous in their raw state to be modeled explicitly by predictive modeling algorithms.

Famous examples include the image, audio, and text data but may just as quickly include tabular data with millions of attributes.

Function extraction is a method that automatically restricts the dimensionality of these types of findings to a much smaller range that can be modeled.

For tabular results, this can involve projection methods such as Principal Component Analysis and unsupervised clustering methods. It can include line or edge detection for image images. Depending on the domain, photo, video, and audio observations are used by several of the same types of DSP approaches.

The secret to the extraction function is that the methods are automated (although they may need to be built and assembled using simplified methods) and solve unmanageably high dimensional records, most generally used for analog observations stored in digital formats.

Feature Selection: from a lot of features to a useful handful

Not all of the functions are made equal.

Those characteristics that do not apply to the issue need to be excluded. There will be certain functionality that will be more relevant to the consistency of the model than others. There may also be functions that are obsolete in the light of other features.

Feature Selection solves these concerns by dynamically choosing a subset that is most helpful to the challenge.

Feature selection algorithms may use a score method to rank and choose features such as correlation or other feature value methods.

More advanced methods may search for subsets of features by trial and error, build and evaluate models automatically to pursue the objectively most predictive subset of features.

Some approaches can be baked in collecting functions or used as a side effect of the model. Stepwise regression is an example of an algorithm that automatically performs the selection of features as part of the model creation process.

Regularization techniques, such as LASSO and ridge regression, can also be known to have feature selection algorithms baked in. They deliberately aim to eliminate or discount the input of features as part of the model construction process.

Learn more on the post: Guide to Feature Collection.

Function Design: Manual construction of new features of raw data

The best outcomes come down to you, the practitioner, to render the features.

Feature value and selection will tell you about the features' empirical usefulness, but they have to come from somewhere.

You need to build them manually. It involves spending a lot of time on real sample data (not aggregates) and thinking about the underlying type of the query, the structure of the data, and how best to expose it to predictive modeling algorithms.

For tabular info, it also means a combination of aggregating or merging features to create new features and decomposing or separating parts to develop new features.

Textual evidence also requires the creation of a document or context-specific metrics that are important to the issue. For image info, it may also mean an immense amount of time prescribing automated filters to choose the correct structures.

It is the part of function engineering that is always the most spoken about as an art form, which is attributed to the significance and signaled as a differentiator in competitive machine learning.

4.2: Spot-Check Algorithm

The Belt Test

You need to describe your evaluation brace. The test harness is the data that you will train and test an algorithm against and the success indicator you will use to determine its performance. It's essential to describe your test harness well so that you can concentrate on testing various algorithms and thinking deeply about the problem.

The purpose of the test harness is to test algorithms quickly and reliably against a fair representation of the problem being resolved. The effect of evaluating several harness algorithms would approximate how some algorithms work against the chosen output assessment on the topic. You would know which algorithms may be worth turning to the problem, which should not be further thought.

The findings will also give you an idea of how palpable the issue is. If some different learning algorithms typically perform poorly on the topic, it may be an example of the lack of structure available to the learning algorithms. It may be because there is simply a lack of learning structure in the chosen results, or it may be an incentive to test out new transformations to reveal the system to learning algorithms.

Measurement of results

Performance assessment is the way you want to test the solution to the problem. It's the calculation you'll make of the assumptions made by a qualified test dataset model.

Quality tests are usually trained in the class of problems you deal with, for example, grouping, regression, and clustering. A variety of standard success metrics will give you a ranking that applies to your problem domain. E.g., the accuracy of classification for classification (total correct correction divided by the real predictions made multiple by 100 to turn it into a percentage).

You would also like to see a more thorough overview of the results; for example, you may want to know about the spam classification topic's false positives since good e-mails would be classified as spam and cannot be read.

There is a range of standard success metrics to pick from. You seldom have to invent a new success metric yourself since you will usually identify or modify one that better captures the issue's needs being tackled. Look at the related problems you have encountered and the success metrics used to see how they can be implemented.

Test and Train Dataset

You would need to choose a test set and a training set from the transformed results. An algorithm will be conditioned on the testing dataset and tested against the test set. It can be as easy as choosing a random data break (66 percent for preparation, 34 percent for testing) or may require more complex sampling methods.

A trained model is not subjected to the test dataset during testing, and any assumptions made on that dataset are meant to suggest the success of the model in general. As such, you want to make sure that the dataset's collection is reflective of the problem you solve.

Cross-validation

A more advanced solution than using a test and train dataset is to use the entire converted dataset to train and test the algorithm. The tool that you might use in your test harness is called cross-validation.

First, it involves splitting the data collection into various similarly broad classes of cases (called folds). The model is then conditioned on all the folds except the one left out, and the prepared model is checked on the left-out fold. The procedure is replicated such that each fold is given the chance to be left out and function as a test dataset. Finally, output metrics are combined with broad ranges to approximate the algorithm's ability to solve the query.

E.g., 3-fold cross-validation will entail practicing and checking the 3-fold model:

#1: Train on folds 1+2, test on folds three #2: train on folds 1+3, test on folds two #3: train on folds 2+3, test on folds 1

The number of folds may vary depending on your dataset's scale, but the specific numbers are 3, 5, 7, and 10 folds. The goal is to have a healthy balance between the size and interpretation of the data in your train set and the test set.

When you're just getting started, stick with a necessary splitting of train and test data (such as 66%/34%) and switch to cross-validation until you have more confidence.

Checking of algorithms

When starting with a problem and identifying a test harness that you're satisfied with, it's time to try out a range of machine learning algorithms. Spot checks are helpful because they help you rapidly see if there are any learning mechanisms in the data and predict which algorithms could successfully deal with the problem.

Spot tests can allow you to sort out any problems with your test harness and ensure that the chosen performance indicator is acceptable.

The best first algorithm to search is a random one. Plug in a random number generator to produce projections within the required range. It should be the worst "algorithm outcome" you have obtained and the criterion against which all progress will be measured.

Choose 5-10 standard algorithms suitable for your problem and run them through your test harness. By regular algorithms, I don't mean any unique setups for formal methods. Reasonable to the problem means that algorithms can tackle regression if you have a regression problem.

Choose approaches from the algorithm groupings that we've already studied. I want to have a diverse mix and have 10-20 different algorithms taken from a wide variety of algorithm types. Depending on the library I'm using, I can see up to 50+ standard methods to quickly flush out promising practices.

If you wish to run many methods, you can need to revisit the data preparation and reduce the scale of your chosen dataset. It can reduce the trust in the findings, so evaluate for different data set sizes. You may want to use a smaller dataset for spot check algorithms and a fuller dataset for algorithm tuning.

Why are you going to be Spot-Check Algorithms for your Machine Learning Problems?

Spot-checking algorithms are about getting a fast evaluation of various algorithms on your machine learning problem, so you know what algorithms to work on and what to discard.

Spot – Checking Algorithms

Spot-checking algorithms are part of the machine learning process used. On a new question, you need to rapidly decide which type or class of algorithms is good at choosing the structure in your problem and which is not.

The alternative to spot checks is that you feel frustrated by an extensive range of algorithms and types of algorithms that you might try to end up trying very little or going for what has worked for you in the past. It results in a waste of time and sub-par results.

Benefits of Spot-Check Algorithms

There are three main advantages of spot-checking algorithms for machine learning problems:

- **Speed:** You might spend a lot of time messing around with various algorithms, tuning parameters, and worrying about what algorithms are doing right to your problem. I've been there because I've ended up trying the same algorithms over and over, and I haven't been systematic. A single spot-check experiment will save hours, days, and even weeks of noodles.
- **Objective:** There is a temptation to do what has worked for you before. We select our favorite algorithm (or algorithms) and add it to any problem we have. The strength of machine learning is that there are too many possible approaches to solve a particular problem. A spot-check experiment helps you to automatically and independently explore the algorithms that are ideally suited to selecting the structure of the problem so that you can center your attention.
- **Results:** You get functional results from spot-checking algorithms quickly. In the first spot trial, you could find a good enough solution. Alternatively, you will soon discover that your dataset does not show enough structure for any mainstream algorithm to perform well. Spot-checking offers you the results you need to determine whether to go forward and refine a given model or back to rethink the issue's presentation.

I think seeing mainstream algorithms on your dilemma is a no-brainer first move.

Spot Tips-Check Algorithms

You can do some things while you're testing algorithms to make sure you have useful and workable results.

Below are five tips to make sure you get the most out of spot-checking machine learning algorithms on your problem.

Diversity of the algorithm: You want to get a decent combination of algorithm styles. I would like to use case-based approaches, functions, and kernels (like neural nets, regression, and SVM), rules (like Decision Table and RIPPER), and decision tree structures (like CART, ID3, and C4.5).

Best of Foot Forward: Any algorithm needs to be offered a chance to get the best foot forward. It does not mean doing a sensitivity analysis of each algorithm's parameters but using tests and heuristics to give each algorithm a reasonable chance. E.g., if the KNN is in a mixture, give it three options with k values of 1, 5, and 7.

Formal Experiment: Don't play the game. There's a massive temptation to try many different things informally, to play around with algorithms on your problem. The idea of spot-checking is to quickly get to the methods that do an excellent job on the problem. Plan the experiment, execute it, and then evaluate the effects. Ome methodical, please. I prefer to rate algorithms by their statistically meaningful wins (in pairwise comparisons) and take the top 3-5 as the basis for tuning.

Jumping off Point: Best-performing algorithms are the starting point, not the solution to the problem. Algorithms that have been proven to be successful may not be the right algorithms for the job. They are more likely to be helpful pointers to the types of algorithms that function well on the problem. E.g., if KNN performs well, imagine follow-up research on all of the instance-based approaches and variants of KNN that you might think of.

Create your shortlist: When you learn and try many different algorithms, you can add new algorithms to the suite of algorithms you use in a spot-check trial. When I discover a stable algorithm setup, I want to generalize it and include it in my suite, making my suite more durable for the next topic.

Start building your suite of spot-checking algorithms.

Top 10 of the algorithms

A paper entitled "Best 10 Algorithms in Data Mining" was written in 2008. Who should have gone past a title like that? It was also translated into a book named "The Best Ten Algorithms in Data Mining" and inspired the structure of another "Machine Learning in Reality."

It could be a nice piece of paper for you to hop and start a shortlist of algorithms to search for the next machine learning problem. The top 10 algorithms for data mining are described below.

- C4.5 This is a decision tree algorithm that involves descending methods such as the popular C5.0 and ID3 algorithms.
- K-means that. It's a clustering algorithm.
- Help for Vector Machines. It is a significant area of analysis.
- Apriori, guy. It is the go-to extraction law algorithm.
- Uh, EM. Along with the k-means, go to the clustering algorithm.
- It's PageRank. I seldom touch on graphic-based topics.
- AdaBoost, guy. It is the family of Ensemble Enhancement Approaches.
- Well, knn (k-nearest neighbor). Comfortable and practical, instance-based process.
- The Naïve Bayes. Comfortable and robust use of Bayes' data theorem.
- CART (Classification and Regression Trees) is another tree-based approach.

How to Select Correct Test Choices to Validate Machine Learning Algorithms

Randomness is the source of the difficulties of selecting the correct test choices. Most (almost) machine learning algorithms use randomness in every way. Randomness may be explicit in the algorithm, or it may be in the data sample chosen to train the algorithm.

It does not mean that algorithms generate unexpected results; they produce results with a certain level of noise or variation. We call this type of small variance stochastic and algorithms that make use of its stochastic algorithms.

Train and analyze with the same data

If you have a dataset, you will want to train the model on the dataset and report the model effects on the dataset. That's how good the model is, isn't it?

The problem with this approach to testing algorithms is that you will indeed know the algorithm's output on the data collection but may not have any idea of how the algorithm will work on data that the model has not been trained on (so-called unseen data).

It is important only if you want to use the model to make assumptions about unseen results.

Break Research

The simple approach to using one dataset for both preparation and predicting the algorithm's output for unseen data is to break the dataset. You take the dataset and split it between the testing dataset and the evaluation dataset. E.g., you randomly pick 66% of the training instances and use the remaining 34% as a test dataset.

The algorithm is run on the training dataset, and the model is generated and validated on the test dataset. You get the accuracy of the results, let's say, 87 percent accuracy of the classification.

Spit tests are fast and great when you have a lot of data or when training a model is expensive (it resources or time) (it resources or time). A split test on an extensive data set will provide a reliable approximation of the algorithm's real performance.

How robust is the data algorithm? Can we honestly assume that the accuracy of 87 percent can be achieved?

The problem is that if we spit the training dataset back into another 66 percent/34% break, we will get a different outcome from our algorithm. It's called the model variance.

Multiple Break Research

The solution to our problem of breaking the test to produce different outcomes on different dataset splits is to reduce the random process variance and do so many times. We will gather the results from a reasonable number of runs (say 10) and take the average.

Let's assume, for example, that we split our dataset 66 percent/34 percent, run our algorithm, and got the precision, and we repeated this ten times with ten different splits. We may have 10 precision scores as follows: 87, 87, 88, 89, 88, 86, 88, 87, 87, 87.

The average output of our model is 87.5, with a standard deviation of approximately 0.85.

The problem with multiple split tests is that it is likely that certain data instances may never be used for training or research, while others might be chosen multiple times. The effect is that it may skew the results and may not give a meaningful idea of the algorithm's accuracy.

Cross-validation

The solution to ensuring that each instance is used for training and testing an equal number of times while reducing the variance of the accuracy of the score is cross-validation. Specifically, k-fold cross-validation, where k is the number of splits to be made in the dataset.

Let's choose a value of k=10, for example (very common). It will split the dataset into ten parts (10 folds), and the algorithm will run ten times. Each time the algorithm is run, 90 percent of the data will be trained, and 10 percent tested, and each algorithm run will change which 10 percent of the algorithm data will be tested.

In this example, each data instance will be used precisely nine times as a training instance and one time as a test instance. Accuracy will not be a mean and a standard deviation but rather an accurate score of how many correct predictions have been made.

The k-fold cross-validation method is the go-to method for evaluating the performance of a dataset algorithm. You want to choose k-values that give you good-sized training and test dataset for your algorithm. Not too disproportionate (too large or small for training or test) (too large or small for practice or trial). If you have a lot of data, you can either collect the data or return to a split exam.

Cross-validation does provide an unbiased estimate of the output of algorithms on unseen results, but what if the algorithm itself uses randomness. The algorithm will yield different results with the same training data every time it was trained with another random number of seeds (start of the sequence of pseudo-randomness). Cross-validation does not allow for uncertainty in the assumptions of the algorithm.

Another point of interest is that cross-validation itself uses randomness to determine how to break the dataset into k-folds. Cross-validation does not predict how the algorithm operates for various sets of folds.

This only matters if you want to consider how stable a dataset algorithm is.

Multiple cross-validations

The way to account for the variation in the algorithm itself is to perform cross-validation several times and take the mean and standard deviation of each run's accuracy.

It will estimate the efficiency of the dataset algorithm and an estimate of how stable (the size of the standard deviation) the performance is.

Suppose you have one mean and one standard deviation for algorithm A and another mean and standard deviation for algorithm B. They vary (for example, algorithm A has higher accuracy). How do you know if the difference is meaningful?

It is only important if you want to compare the results between algorithms.

Statistical Meaning

The approach for evaluating algorithm output assessments using different sequences of k-fold cross-validation is the use of statistical significance measures (like the Student's t-test).

The outcomes of several k-fold cross-validation sequences are a list of numbers. We would like to summaries all numbers using the mean and the standard deviation. You may think of these figures as a snapshot of the underlying population. The statistical significance test asks the question: are two samples taken from the same people? (no difference). Suppose the answer is "yes," so even if the mean and the standard deviations are different, the variance may be assumed not to be statistically significant.

We may use statistical significance tests to clarify discrepancies (or lack of) between algorithm outcomes when multiple runs are used (like multiple runs of k-fold cross-validation with different random number seeds). It can happen when we try to make accurate assumptions about the findings (algorithm A was better than algorithm B and the difference was statistically significant)

It is not the end of the matter since there are different statistical validity measures (parametric and nonparametric) and criteria for these tests (p-value). I'm going to draw a line here because if you've been with me this long, you know enough about choosing research choices to yield comprehensive (publishable) outcomes.

4.3: Improve Results

The way to start is to get better results from algorithms that you already know are doing well on your problem. You will do this by experimenting and fine-tuning the setup for these algorithms.

Machine learning algorithms are parameterized, and the adjustment of these parameters will affect the learning process's outcome. Think of each algorithm parameter as a graph dimension with the given parameter values as a point along the axis. Three parameters will be a cube of possible algorithm configurations, and n-parameters would be an n-dimensional hypercube of possible algorithm configurations.

The goal of algorithm tuning is to find the best point or points for your problem in that hypercube. You'll be optimizing against your test harness, but again you can't underestimate the value of investing time developing a trusted test harness.

You can address this search issue by using automatic methods that position a grid on the possibility of space and a sample where a successful algorithm configuration is available. You can then use specific points in an optimization algorithm to zoom in to the optimal results.

You should replicate this experiment with various well-functioning approaches and discover the most you can do with any of them. I highly suggest that the procedure be automatic and fairly rough-grained. You can easily hit points of decreased returns (fractional percentage improvement in performance) which might not be converted into the production system.

The more the algorithm parameters are tuned, the more biased the algorithm will be for the testing data and the evaluation harness. This technique can be successful, but it can also lead to more vulnerable models that exceed your test harness and do not work well in reality.

Ensembles

The Ensemble Methods are concerned with integrating the effects of several methods to obtain better results. Ensemble approaches perform best when you have several "reasonable enough" models specializing in various sections of the problem.

It can be done in a variety of ways. Three range of techniques that you can explore are:

- **Bagging:** Described more formally as Bootstrapped Aggregation, the same algorithm has different viewpoints on the problem from being conditioned on different training data subsets.
- **Boosting:** Different algorithms are conditioned on the same training results.
- **Blending:** Defined more formally as Layered Generalization or Stacking is where some models whose predictions are used as feedback into a new model know how to blend predictions into overall projections.

It's a smart idea to get into the Ensemble Methods after you've exhausted more conventional methods. There are two good reasons for this; they are usually more complicated than traditional methods. The traditional techniques give you the right base level on which you can expand and develop your ensembles.

Extreme Engineering Feature

The previous two methods looked at bringing more out of machine learning algorithms. This approach is about exposing more structure to the issue of learning algorithms. We learned about attribute decomposition and aggregation in data processing to help normalize data for machine learning algorithms. We bring the notion to the edge in this approach. I name this approach intense feature engineering when the word "feature engineering" will suffice.

Think of the data as having dynamic multidimensional constructs embedded in it that machine learning algorithms know how to identify and use to make decisions. You want to open these systems to algorithms better so that algorithms can do their best. The challenge is that some of these systems can be too dense or too complex for algorithms to be identified without support. You may already have some knowledge of these systems from your domain experience.

Take attributes and decompose them into different features. Technically, what you're doing with this approach is that dependences and nonlinear relationships to more comfortable, more independent, linear relationships.

It may be a foreign thought, so here are examples:

Machine Learning

Category: You have a categorical attribute with the values [red, green blue]; you might break it into three binary characteristics of red, green, and blue and give 1 or 0 for each case.

Right: You have a real-valued quantity with values ranging from 0 to 1000. You could generate ten binary attributes, each representing a bin of values (0-99 for bin 1, 100-199 for bin 2, etc.), and assign a binary value (1/0) for containers to each case.

I suggest that you execute this procedure one step at a time, create a new test/train dataset for each change you make, and test algorithms on the dataset. It will provide you with an intuition of attributes and features in the database that reveal more or less knowledge of algorithms and effects on performance measurement. You may use these findings to direct more intense decomposition or aggregation.

Improve Data Output

You will win big with improvements to the training data and problem description. Perhaps the most significant wins.

Strategy: Generate fresh and diverse viewpoints on the data to better show the underlying problem's structure to the learning algorithms.

The Data Tactic

Get more detail. Will you get more or better data on quality? New nonlinear machine learning strategies such as deep learning continue to boost efficiency with more results.

Invent More Info. If you can't get more data, can you make new data? You will incorporate or permute existing data or use a probabilistic model to produce new data.

Clean up your files. Will you boost your data signal? Perhaps there are missed or corrupt observations that can be fixed or deleted or outlier values within acceptable limits that can be set or removed to increase your results' accuracy.

Resamples the results. Can you re-sample data to change the size or distribution of the data? You may be able to use a much smaller sample of data for your experiments to speed up or over-sample or under-sample observations of a specific type to represent them in your dataset better.

Reframe Your Problem: Can you change the type of prediction problem you're going to solve? Reframe your data as a regression, binary or multiclass classification, time series, anomaly detection, rating, recommendation, etc.

Please rescale your info. Will you rescale the numerical input variables? Normalization and standardization of input data result in an improvement in algorithms' performance using weighted inputs or distance measurements.

Turn your info. Can you reshape the distribution of your data? Making input data more Gaussian or going through an exponential function may reveal data features to a learning algorithm.

Project Your Data: Can you project your data to a lower-dimensional area? You may use an unsupervised clustering or prediction approach to construct your dataset's brand-new compact image.

Selection of functions. Are all input variables just as important? Using feature discovery and feature value approaches to build new data views to experiment using modeling algorithms.

Function Tech. Can you build and apply new functionality to your data? There may be attributes that can be broken down into several new values (such as categories, dates, or strings) or attribute that can be aggregated to indicate an occurrence.

Improving output of algorithms

Machine learning is about algorithms.

Strategy: Classify algorithms and data representations that are above the output baseline and above the average. Keep cynical about outcomes and concept tests that make it impossible to fool yourself.

Algorithmic Tactics

Form of re-sampling. What method of re-sampling is used to estimate the abilities of the latest data? Using a technique and setup that makes the most of the available data. The k-fold cross-validation approach with a holdout data set may be the best practice.

Metric Assessment. What is the criterion used to test the ability of predictions? Using a metric that better captures the challenge and domain specifications. It's certainly not the consistency of classification.

Simple results. What is the simple performance of evaluating algorithms? Using a random algorithm or a zero-rule algorithm (predicted mean or mode) to set the baseline to rank all of the algorithms being assessed.

Spot Linear Algorithms Check. What are linear algorithms running well? Linear models are also more biased, easy to understand, and simple to train. They are favored if you can produce positive results. Test some linear processes.

Spot Check Non-linear Algorithms. What are nonlinear algorithms running well? Nonlinear algorithms also need more input, are more complicated, but can provide better performance. Test some nonlinear techniques.

The Steal in Literature. What algorithms have been documented in the literature to function well on your problem? You may have ideas of algorithm forms or extensions of classical methods to explore your dilemma.

The Standard Configurations. What are the typical configurations of the algorithms being evaluated? Each algorithm needs an opportunity to do an excellent job of dealing with your dilemma. It doesn't mean to tune the parameters (yet), but it does point to explore how to set up each algorithm well and give it a chance to fight back in the bake-off algorithm.

Improve the output with tuning algorithm

Algorithm tuning will be where you spend much of your time. It could be time-consuming. Typically, one or two well-performing algorithms can be found easily by spot-checking. Having the best out of these algorithms will take days, weeks, or months.

Strategy: Get the best out of the efficient machine learning algorithms.

Tactics of Tuning

Diagnosis. What kind of diagnostics do you and your algorithm review? You will want to analyze the learning curves and see if the solution is over or under-fitting the problem and correct it. Different algorithms may offer other visualizations and diagnoses. Check out if the computer is forecasting right and wrong.

Try that instinct. What is your gut telling you? If you have long enough parameters and the feedback cycle is short, you can develop an intuition on configuring an algorithm for a problem. Check this out and see how you can develop a different parameter set up to try on your larger test harness.

The Steal in Literature. What parameters or sets of parameters are used in the literature? Evaluating the efficiency of standard parameters is an excellent place to launch some tuning operations.

Machine Learning

It's a random quest. What conditions will a random search be used? You will be able to use a random search of algorithm hyperparameters to reveal configurations that you might never imagine you would attempt.

Search the grid. What criteria should be used to scan the grid? There may be grids of typical hyperparameter values that you may list to find useful configurations and repeat the procedure for more delicate and more nuanced grids.

Optimize it. What parameters can you customize for? There may be parameters such as structure or learning rate tuned by direct search (like pattern search) or stochastic optimization (like a genetic algorithm).

Alternate implementation. What are other algorithm implementations available? Perhaps an alternative version of the approach will produce a better performance on the same data. Each algorithm has a multitude of micro-decisions that the algorithm implementer needs to make. Some of these decisions may affect the ability of your dilemma.

Extensions of the algorithm. What are the popular algorithm extensions? You may be able to improve efficiency by testing common or regular method extensions. It will include work on implementation.

Customizations of the algorithm. What customizations can be made of the algorithm for your particular case? You may make improvements to the data algorithm, from loss function, internal optimization approaches to individual algorithm decisions.

Ask the specialists. What are the algorithm experts advising in your case? Write a brief e-mail summarizing the prediction dilemma and what you've been attempting to do with one or more expert algorithm scholars. It could expose leading-edge work or scholarly work previously unknown to you with new or fresh ideas.

Outcome: You should have a shortlist of highly tuned algorithms on your machine learning problem, maybe even just one.

Boost output with the package

You can blend the forecasts of several models. After algorithm tuning, this is the next significant field for development. In reality, you can always obtain good results by integrating the predictions of multiple "good enough" models rather than multiple finely tuned (and fragile) models.

Strategy: Incorporate the forecasts of a variety of well-performing models.

Tactical Ensemble

Mix the model projections. Will you specifically integrate the forecasts of different models? You may want to use the same or other algorithms to create several versions. Take the mean or mode from the estimates of a variety of well-performing models.

Mix the data representations. Can you merge forecasts from models that have been conditioned on various data representations? You may have several different estimates of the problem that can be used to train well-performing algorithms, the predictions of which can then be merged.

Mix the data samples. Can you combine models that have been educated on various views of your data? You will be able to build several subsamples of your training data and train a well-performing algorithm, then merge your predictions. It is called bootstrap accumulation or bagging and works well when each model's forecasts are skillful but in different ways (uncorrelated).

Fix the forecasts. Could you correct the assumptions of well-functioning models? You may be able to directly correct forecasts or use a tool such as boosting to learn how to correct prediction errors.

Know how to combine. Will you use a new model to learn how to integrate the forecasts of various well-performing models better? It is called layered generalization or stacking, which also works best because sub models are smart but in various ways, and the aggregator model is an essential linear weighting of predictions. This method can be replicated in several layers of depth.

Outcome: You should have one or more sets of well-performing models that outperform any single model.

Chapter 5: Advantages and Disadvantages of Machine Learning

Have you ever talked of how bright your e-mail inbox is in that it can delete spam, tag critical e-mails or conversations, and segregate advertising, social, and primary messages? In this book, we will clarify how Machine Learning algorithms operate and how we can use them for software development companies' good.

There is a complex algorithm for this form of prediction, and this algorithm is part of the broad range of Machine Learning. The algorithm evaluates the words in the subject line, the connections used in the e-mail, and the receiver list trends. This approach is undoubtedly helping the e-mail provider sector, and such predictive and prescriptive algorithms will benefit all kinds of businesses. But first, let's describe precisely what Machine Learning (ML) is.

Machine Learning is a concise way of often interpreting personal data and numbers and then extracting useful knowledge from this raw dataset. The computational approach that algorithms use can help solve complex data-rich market problems.

Machine learning models are also very adaptable as they begin to learn as new data is entered. It means that the more they live, the more reliable their forecasts are.

Machine Learning algorithms, powered by emerging computational technology, can help increase business scalability and improve business processes when it comes to business. It is solved by incorporating artificial intelligence and business analytics—this is how machine learning can be a solution to some business complexities. Today, ML models are used to forecast everything from web traffic fluctuations, hardware glitches, traffic flows, epidemic outbreaks, stocks, and goods.

The Importance of Algorithm

Machine Learning uses a method where the computer algorithm detects a pattern in the data and forecasts the possible outcomes. Machine learning patterns are highly adaptable in the way they are continuously updated as new data is reached.

As we have stated, the longer they work, this factor makes them more reliable in their forecasts. On the other hand, in business words, a machine learning algorithm combined with emerging computational technology such as artificial intelligence and business analysis may be a solution to various business complexities. It will also help to boost company operations and growth.

A vast number of machines learning algorithms have gained significant attention in the market research community. There has been a substantial boom in machine learning due to expanded volumes, convenient access to data, low-cost computing processing, and rational data storage. Organizations will also benefit from understanding to apply machine learning technologies to their business processes.

With the aid of machine learning, companies can derive large quantities of useful knowledge from raw data. If correctly executed, machine learning can be key to some market challenges and forecast complex consumer behaviors.

5.1: Benefits of Machine Learning

Machine learning and artificial intelligence have created a great deal of buzz in the business sector. Marketers and business analysts are curious to know the benefits and applications of machine learning in business.

Most people have heard about ML and Artificial Intelligence algorithms. But they don't know what it is and its applications.

You need to know the business problems it can solve to use the ML in Business.

Machine learning extracts meaningful information from raw data and delivers accurate results. And this information helps to solve complex and data-rich problems. Machine learning algorithms also learn from and process data. Without being programmed to do so, the technique is used to find different insights.

The ML is evolving quickly and driven by new technologies. It also helps businesses to improve global scalability and business operations for companies.

Recently, many top-ranking companies like Google, Amazon, and Microsoft have adopted machine learning in their business. And they've launched cloud machine learning platforms.

Also, we use Machine Learning in our everyday lives, even without it.

Well, know it. Spam identification by the e-mail provider and photograph, Facebook face tagging included as the primary examples of this application.

There are many advantages of the use of machine learning in the industry. In this post, I'm going to understand why Machine Learning is essential for your company.

Benefits of Business Machine Learning

Here are some of the top advantages that make Machine Learning the best for you.

Business.

Real-Time Company Decision

Any business enterprise relies on the information it gets by analyzing the results. The companies have some important data. But it is difficult to extract the correct information and make a decision from the data. Machine learning uses ML algorithms. It also learns from existing data. The results help businesses to make the right decision. It enables organizations to transform data into knowledge and actionable intelligence. Information can be integrated into day-to-day business processes. These processes then deal with changes in market demands and business circumstances. Business organizations can take advantage of machine learning in this way. It keeps them on top of their competitors.

Simplifies product marketing and helps to predict incorrect sales

ML is helping businesses to promote their products on many platforms. And it's making an accurate forecast of sales. It also offers many advantages to

Companies and helping them in many ways.

Massive consumption of data from unlimited sources

Machine learning consumes a large amount of data for better results. Consumed data is also reviewed and modified for sales and marketing strategies. It gives results based on patterns of customer behavior.

Once the model training is completed, the variables will be identified. Then you'll get accurate data feeds by neglecting deep integration.

Predicting and processing

The speed of ML in consuming data and identifying relevant data is high. It helps you in making the correct decision at the right time. E.g., ML would maximize the customer's best bid.

The customer will then be able to see the offer made when they were interested. So, you don't need to invest your time in planning or making the right advertisement visible to them.

Interpret previous consumer actions

Previous customer behavior helps to make predictions for customers. ML will analyze the data on past behavior and interpret the results.

Easy detection of spam

Spam detection is one of ML's most challenging problems a few years ago. E-mail providers also use rules-based techniques to filter out spam. However, with the help of ML, spam filters are making new rules to eliminate spam e-mails. It helps the network deal with the spam issue. The system recognizes phishing messages and junk mail worldwide.

Improving the efficiency of predictive maintenance

Manufacturers usually follow preventive and corrective maintenance practices. Some of them are often costly and less efficient. However, as ML reaches the market, businesses use ML to search useful observations and trends concealed in the results.

This method is often referred to as predictive maintenance. It helps to reduce unnecessary costs. It also negotiates uncertainties associated with unintended errors. The ML architecture for predictive maintenance includes some of the components described below.

- Workflow Visualization Platform
- The flexible setting for research
- Historical knowledge
- The feedback loops

Improve the consistency of financial rules and templates

The banking market is the largest industry sector. ML has a very positive effect on this market. It also offers programs to boost economic development.

The finance sector's advantages are portfolio optimization, algorithmic trading, fraud prevention, and credit underwriting. ML also offers data assessments for the study and identification of problems. It increases the accuracy of financial rules and templates.

Recommend the best products

For a valid sales and marketing strategy, the product recommendation is as follows:

- It is a vital role. ML models examine consumer buying history and, based on their analysis, classify items of interest to consumers.
- The algorithm also detects secret patterns between objects and seeks related products in classes and clusters. The method is known as unsupervised learning.

And it's also a particular type of ML algorithm. Such models allow businesses to make effective product decisions for their consumers and improve their profits.

Enhance protection and efficiency of the network

Growth in the company. Organizations involve the maintenance of network security and can take the appropriate measures to do so. They must detect undue networking activity before the intrusion enters into full force attack and leak data or impacts services.

Also, machine learning helps to monitor anomalies in the network's actions and performs these steps automatically. As ML is a self-training algorithm, it adapts improvements and eliminates manual testing and analysis. In this way, security-related insights are revealed and help to enhance cybersecurity.

These benefits of ML can extend to a variety of business cases. The primary use of this technology is where manual business operations replace data. All businesses are moving towards machine learning technologies for better outcomes and development.

Simplifies Commodity Promotion and Help for Reliable Revenue Predictions

ML allows businesses in various areas to market their goods further and make reliable revenue predictions. ML gives tremendous benefits to the sales and marketing business, the main ones being-

Consumption of mass data from infinite sources

ML absorbs nearly infinite volumes of detailed data. The data you consume will also be used to continuously analyze and change your sales and marketing plans based on consumer behavior trends. Once the model has been educated, it will be able to recognize crucial variables. As a result, you will be able to get tailored data feeds by preceding lengthy and complicated integrations.

Prediction and Processing of Accelerated Analysis

The pace at which ML consumes data and determines the applicable data makes it possible for you to take suitable action at the right time. E.g., ML can maximize the customer's best subsequent bid. As a result, the consumer would be able to see the correct deal at a given point in time, without necessarily spending time to prepare to make the right ad available to the consumers.

Interpret Previous Consumer Actions

ML would help you to evaluate and interpret data relevant to previous actions or outcomes. Therefore, based on fresh and different evidence, you will make better forecasts of consumer behavior.

Facilitates correct medical forecasts and diagnostics

ML aids in the fast detection of high-risk patients in the healthcare sector, makes near-perfect diagnostics, proposes the right available drugs, and forecasts readbacks. These are mostly focused on the available datasets of anonymous health reports and the signs they display. Nearly effective diagnosis and better medication guidelines would make it possible for people to heal more efficiently without extraneous drugs. In this way, ML makes it possible to improve patient welfare at a reduced cost in the medical field.

Read an essay on Healthcare Machine Learning and Big Data.

Simplifies Time-Intensive Data Entry Reporting

Data replication and inaccuracy are the main problems facing organizations that wish to simplify their data entry method. Well, this condition can be significantly enhanced by statistical models and machine learning algorithms. Through this, robots will handle time-intensive data entry operations, leaving the professional resources free to work on other value-added tasks.

Improves the accuracy of financial rules and templates

ML also has a significant effect on the banking market. Some of the popular machine learning advantages in finance include portfolio management, algorithmic trading, credit underwriting, and, most notably, fraud detection. According to the future of Underwriting' study released by Ernst and Young, ML enables continuous data evaluation for the identification and analysis of irregularities and complexities. It tends to boost the consistency of financial models and rules.

Easy detection of spam

Spam detection was one of the first problems ML had solved. A few years ago, e-mail providers used rules-based techniques to filter out spam. However, with the advent of ML, spam filters are making new rules using brain-like neural networks to eliminate spam mail. Neural networks recognize phishing messages and junk mail by evaluating practices across a vast network of computers.

Increases the efficiency of predictive maintenance in the manufacturing sector

Manufacturing firms have both corrective and preventive maintenance practices in place. However, they are often costly and inefficient. It is where ML can be of great help. ML helps in the development of highly efficient predictive maintenance plans. Following such predictive maintenance plans, the chances of unexpected failures will be minimized, reducing unnecessary preventive maintenance activities.

Best Customer Segmentation and Accurate Lifetime Value Prediction

Customer segmentation and lifetime value prediction are the significant challenges facing marketers today. Sales and marketing units will have vast amounts of relevant data from various channels, such as lead data, website visitors, and e-mail campaigns. However, accurate predictions of incentives and individual marketing offers can be easily achieved with ML. Savvy marketers are now using ML to eliminate the guesswork associated with data-driven marketing. For example, using the behavioral pattern data of a particular set of users during the trial period will help businesses predict the likelihood of conversion to a paid version. Such a model triggers customer intervention to engage customers in the trial better and persuade customers to convert early.

Recommend the best product

Brand advice is an essential part of any sales and marketing campaign, including up-selling and cross-selling. ML models will analyze the customer's purchase history and will identify those products from your product inventory that the customer is interested in. The algorithm would find secret patterns between objects and then organize related products into clusters. This method is known as unsupervised learning, a particular form of ML algorithm. Such a model would allow organizations to make effective product decisions for their consumers, thus motivating goods. In this way, unsupervised learning aims to build a superior product-based recommendation framework.

Easily distinguish themes and patterns.

Machine Learning can review large volumes of data and discover specific trends and patterns that would not be visible to humans. For example, an e-commerce website like Amazon helps to understand the browsing behaviors and purchase its users' history to help cater to the right products, deals, and reminders relevant to them. The results are used to reveal relevant advertisements to them.

No human intervention is needed (automation)

With ML, you don't need to take care of your project every step of the way. Because it involves allowing computers the opportunity to read, it helps them make decisions and develop algorithms independently. Anti-virus tech is a typical example of this; they learn how to filter emerging risks once recognized. ML is excellent at detecting spam, too.

Continuous enhancement

As ML algorithms gain expertise, they continue to increase accuracy and performance. It helps them to make smart choices. Say you need to make a model for weather forecasting. If the amount of data you've kept increasing, the algorithms learn to make more reliable predictions faster.

Managing multidimensional and multi-variety data

Machine Learning algorithms are excellent at processing multidimensional and multi-variety data and can do so in complex or unpredictable settings.

Width Implementations

You may be an e-tailer or health care provider and make ML function for you. Where appropriate, it can help provide a more intimate service to consumers but still reaching the right customers.

5.2: Disadvantages of Machine Learning

With all the benefits of its strength and success, Machine Learning is not ideal. The following considerations are used to restrict it:

The acquisition of data

Machine Learning needs large data sets to practice, inclusive/unbiased, and of high quality. There will also be occasions where they have to wait for new data to be produced.

Time and Money

ML requires enough time to let the algorithms learn and grow enough to serve their purpose with a high degree of accuracy and relevance. It still requires colossal capital to run. It can mean extra computing power requirements for you.

Interpreting the findings

Another big problem is the ability to analyze algorithm-generated data correctly. You will need to select the algorithms for your function carefully.

Strong error-responsibility

Machine Learning is autonomous but somewhat error-prone. Suppose you train a data set algorithm that is minimal enough not to be inclusive. You wind up with biased forecasts resulting from a bias preparation package. It leads to meaningless commercials being presented to consumers. In the case of ML, such bugs will cause a sequence of errors that can be undetected for an extended time. And when they're detected, it takes quite a while to identify the cause of the problem and much longer fix it.

As a result, we researched the Benefits and Drawbacks of Machine Learning. Often, it lets people understand that they need to choose machine learning. Although Machine Learning can be extremely useful when applied correctly and in the right place (where large training data sets are available), it is not for everybody.

Conclusion

Machine learning is rapidly growing in the field of computer science. It has applications in almost every other area of study. It is already commercially implemented because machine learning can solve problems that are too difficult or time-consuming for humans to solve. To describe machine learning in general terms, various models are used to learn patterns in data and make accurate predictions based on the ways it observes.

First, I introduced generalization and over-fitting. Both of these topics are linked to supervised learning, which uses training data to train the model. Abstraction is when a machine learning model can accurately predict results from data that it has not seen before. Overfitting occurs when a model learns training data too well and cannot generalize. Underfitting, the opposite of overfitting, can also happen with supervised learning. With under-fitting, the model is unable to make accurate predictions with both training data and new data.

Then I was talking about datasets. With supervised learning, data is divided into three groups: train, dev, and test datasets. The dataset of the train is used to train the model. The dev dataset is used to validate the model during model creation but not during model testing. The test dataset is used until the model is complete to see how it responds to data that it has never seen before. I also discussed how to select the relevant fields in a dataset. Often information is not essential and should not be included in the data collection.

After that, I looked at artificial neural networks. Neural networks have three layers: an input, a hidden layer, and a display layer. Each layer consists of nodes. The layers are connected to the vectors. Neural networks were one of the first machine learning models to be developed, and many variations in neural networks were explored.

Next, I'm thinking of deep neural networks. Where artificial neural networks have one hidden layer, deep neural networks have multiple hidden layers. Due to multiple hidden layers' complexity, deep neural networks are better suited to some tasks than simple neural networks. However, their added complexity makes it more difficult for them to train.

Last, I'm talking about evolutionary neural networks. Again, this is a simple neural network variation. The benefit of using a evolutionary neural network is that it is designed to manage image and speech recognition tasks better. Instead of hidden layers, the evolutionary neural networks have a evolutionary and pooling layer. Because of these layers, evolutionary neural networks are preferred for image and speech recognition.

Thank you very much for reading the book. I haven't even scratched the surface of anything I should talk about with machine learning, so I hope this will introduce some of the topics in this area. It's going to be interesting to see where machine learning is going in the next 20 years and how it's going to transform our life for the better.

Printed in Great Britain
by Amazon